RED FLAG!

DO YOU KNOW WHEN YOU'RE BEING PLAYED?

SONEAKQUA J. WHITE

RED FLAG!

Copyright © 2018 by Soneakqua J. White.

All rights reserved.

No part of this book may be reproduced or transmitted in any form or by any means, electronic or mechanical, including photocopying, recording, or by any information storage and retrieval system, without permission in writing from the copyright author, except for the use of brief quotations in a book review.

Published in the United States by
Pen2Pad Ink Publishing.

Requests to publish work from this book or to contact the author should be sent to:
sjw@atthetablecounseling.com

Soneakqua J. White retains the rights to all images

Interior design: Pen2Pad Ink Publishing

DISCLAIMER

This book has been written for educational purposes only. It provides information only up to the publishing date therefore this book should be used as a guidance tool and not an ultimate source. Its purpose is to provide information but does not contain all information on the subject. More research on your part may be needed. Every effort has been made to make this book as accurate as possible. The author and publisher shall have no liability or responsibility to any person or entity regarding any loss or damage incurred, or alleged to have incurred, directly or indirectly, by the information contained in this book.

RED FLAG!

CONTENTS

Introduction 11

Part I: Being Played By A Person

Section I: Manipulation 15
Section II: Abuse 37
Subsection

    A. Physical Abuse 39
    B. Verbal Abuse 59
    C. Mental/Emotional Abuse 77
    D. Sexual Abuse 91
    E. Spiritual Abuse 109
    F. Self-Harm 127

Part II: Being Played By Your Mind

Triggers Section I: Past Events/Trauma 143
Section II: Senses 167
Subsection

    A. Sight 171
    B. Sound 181
    C. Smell 193
    D. Taste 205
    E. Touch 213
    F. Intuition 225

Message From the Author 233
About the Author 235
Other Books By Soneakqua J. White 237
Resources 239

RED FLAG!

KEY TO ICONS

 RED FLAG

 TRIGGER

INTRODUCTION

The working definition of a Red Flag! in this book is a warning. We should take heed to the flags in order to avoid or get out of a potentially painful situation. However, there are occasions where the Red Flag! is a signal for you to step back and evaluate before you walk into something you cannot escape. There are some flags that are obvious and some that are not. As a therapist, I do not assume that my clients see things the way I see them. I always try and point it out. Decision making becomes an important skill to have. The realization that everyone has rights is of utmost importance.

Individuals who come from abusive pasts often miss flags because they are familiar with potentially dangerous encounters. This is where recognition becomes difficult. A person who has grown up in or around abuse may not see it as such. This in no way indicates that they find it enjoyable. It simply means they have come to know it as normal.

This book breaks down real life examples. Please understand that each Red Flag! can stand alone or it could be combined with other flags. You will see how this works in upcoming scenarios. The examples you will see here by no means represents an exhaustive list. Do not disregard any of these cases simply because it is not *exactly* what happened to you. If any Red Flag! raises even a hint of a question in your mind, you need help.

Please read through to the end of this book. The last page contains resources that will help anyone who discovers they are in a situation they need to get out of. Do not take this lightly. It may not be for you, but I am almost certain you know someone who will benefit from it.

RED FLAG!

PART I
BEING PLAYED BY A PERSON

RED FLAG!

Section #1: Manipulation

What is manipulation? Merriam-Webster gives one definition for manipulation as to control or play upon by artful, unfair, or insidious means especially to one's own advantage.

Who gets chosen to be manipulated? Someone who is deemed as an easy target. You will be tested and you only need to fall for the scam once to become a constant mark.

Why are certain people good targets? These are likely kind or soft-hearted individuals who feel a sense of shame, guilt, rejection, misplaced responsibility, a need to be loved or accepted, etc. A good target could also be someone who is simply unsuspecting.

Characteristics of a manipulator:
A manipulator is usually a crafty person who is deliberate in his or her actions. Typically, well-liked by many, the manipulator gets to know a potential target. He or she needs to find out your weaknesses in order to use them against you consistently.

How does one recognize, avoid and/or escape manipulation?

Recognize: Do NOT ignore your own thoughts and feelings. You know when something doesn't sit well with you. Pay attention to what that "gut check" is telling you. Are you feeling used, fooled, tricked, guilty, obligated, etc.? Are you wondering "why can't they or won't they do this for themselves?" Are you putting your life on hold and taking care of the needs of others before yours? Do you feel selfish or like a bad person for wanting to say "no"?

Avoid or Escape: Please know that you have the right to say "no" because you matter too. After you recognize that you are possibly being manipulated you must take action. Remember that you are not responsible for changing the manipulator. You are only responsible for changing your actions toward them. Your thoughts and feelings are the Red Flags. Ask yourself why you are doing what you are doing for the manipulator. If it is for any other reason than "because I want to or because they are incapable and I need to help", then you should re-evaluate. If you are doing something out of guilt, obligation, force, etc. you are likely being manipulated.

This next section gives real life examples of manipulation. It also includes highlights of potential Red Flags that are often missed in situations such as these. You may not have found

RED FLAG!

yourself being taken advantage of, but I guarantee you know someone who has.

SONEAKQUA J. WHITE

RED FLAG!

Scenario #1:

Target: "Hey Sis! I'm at the store and I see this cute shirt for $8! Do you think I should get it to wear to my office Christmas party?"

Manipulator: "You don't have anything else you can wear to the party?" 🚩 #1

Target: "Not anything nice. I kind of wanted something new so I would look as nice as everyone else."

Manipulator: "Well, you know we don't have much food in the house." 🚩 #2

Target: "Why not? I just gave you $40 for food." 🚩 #3

Manipulator: "I know but it's four of us over here. You know food don't last long. All you have to worry about is yourself. I got a husband and two kids. If I didn't have the kids I would just go without eating." 🚩 #4

Target: "Well, I might be able to find something cheaper than $8. Let me keep looking."

Manipulator: "Why don't you just wear something you already have? I might have to ask you for that money. You know it's almost Christmas. Ain't you coming over here to eat?" 🚩 #5

Target: "You're right. I'll just take this money and get ya'll some groceries. I don't even need to go to the Christmas party."

Manipulator: "Don't get the groceries yet because you don't know what we need. Just bring me the money." 🚩 #6

RED FLAG EXPLANATIONS:

🚩 #1: "You don't have anything else you can wear to the party?" She is being asked if she has something else to wear for a reason. This is a feeler question because the answer to this question tells her sister how to lead into what she wants. So what if she does have something else she can wear to the party? Does working every day not give her the right to buy what she wants? Why is she allowing her sister to question her about how she spends her money? That's the better question.

🚩 #2: "Well, you know we don't have much food

RED FLAG!

in the house." Pretend this is you. What does your sister's household not having food have to do with you? This is a guilt trip. The sister feels you shouldn't be out buying clothes when she doesn't have food. She is getting ready to make her problem your problem. It's not that you shouldn't care about the fact that she doesn't have food. The issue is that she is getting ready to lay the burden on you. She has two incomes to your one. This is an issue of money management. What she does not tell you is that the reason there is no food in her house is because she bought liquor, weed and got her nails done.

🚩 #3: "Why not? I just gave you $40 for food." You just gave her money. Apparently, this is the norm for you to supply your sister's household with food and/or money. You just gave her $40 and she is questioning you spending $8? You gave her more than you wanted to spend on yourself.

🚩 #4: "I know but it's four of us over here. You know food don't last long. All you have to worry about is yourself. I got a husband and two kids. If I didn't have the kids I would just go without eating." Wow! A single woman taking care of her sister's entire family! She has a husband but is asking for money from her little sister. If you have not figured out that you're being taken advantage of yet, here is your newsflash. This family apparently has a problem with managing money and you have become their savior. She knows you would never allow the children to suffer so you have made it easy for her to play on your sympathy. Guilt is a very strong motivator and your sister has found your weakness.

🚩 **#5:** "Why don't you just wear something you already have? I might have to ask you for that money. You know it's almost Christmas. Ain't you coming over here to eat?" You cannot buy an $8 shirt because your sister might have to ask you for your money. After all, if you're coming over to eat then you need to pull your weight. She couldn't possibly feed you considering everything you've done for her. If you're coming over then you need to ensure there is enough food for you and the rest of the family.

🚩 **#6:** "Don't get the groceries yet because you don't know what we need. Just bring me the money." This statement is how you know you're being played. Throughout the majority of the conversation your sister made her case about the family not having food. Now, she does not want you to buy food. She just wants the money. This entire conversation was to keep you from spending money on yourself so she could get you to give it to her. You not only gave up buying a shirt, but you've also decided to miss out on a

RED FLAG!

Christmas party that you were looking forward to.

What is the manipulation? This older sister feels like her little sister has the money and because she is single she does not need it. The older sister has also gotten used to using the little sister in this manner so she does not think twice about manipulating her. She does not have to learn how to manage her money any better because she has figured out where she can get more from. She and her husband both work and the children are working age as well. But, it's much easier to get it from her little sister because she is so willing to sacrifice her own happiness to give.

Why would a sibling treat another sibling in this way? Entitlement comes into play in this scenario. The older sister feels that since her younger sister apparently has the money and has been willing to give it, then she should continue to do so. She has learned to play on her sympathy. Who wants to hear about children going hungry if you can do something about it? In this instance, the older sister does not care how her behavior affects her little sister. All she is concerned about is what she can get. She doesn't really even think about how her little sister feels.

How does the little sister recognize and avoid being a target again? She must realize that she is being used. If she can look at the situation for what it really is instead of feeling obligated and guilty, she will be able to take her hands off. There are four people in her sister's home who are perfectly capable of working. There is only one of her. She must return the responsibility of her sister's family back to her sister instead of trying to save them. It may sound cruel but if they go hungry once, they will likely figure out how to ensure that a four-income household always has food. There is no reason why they shouldn't. It's not that the little sister cannot help her family, but it should not come out of guilt. She will need to excuse herself from being responsible for any of her sister's problems. If you do not get a handle on this type of manipulation you will never be free of it. The children are growing up watching these interactions. If they see you catering to their mother in this way, they may begin to feel like they should be able to do the same thing. Then you have another generation looking to you to take care of them. No one becomes responsible.

RED FLAG!

Scenario #2:

Manipulator: "What do you want for your birthday and Christmas?"

Target: "An iPad!"

Manipulator: "The lady brought me an iPad mini so I sent it back." 🚩 #1

Target: "Dad, since you didn't get me the iPad can you just get me a storm door for my house? I close in May."

Manipulator: "Ok. Find the one you want and order it. We need somebody with a truck so we can pick it up." 🚩 #2

Target: "Ok Dad, we're supposed to pick up the door tomorrow so you can put in on. My friend is going to meet us at the store with the truck. He can help you too. We're still on right?"

Manipulator: "Yep. Call me in the morning and wake me up."

Target: "Good morning Dad, my friend has something to do this morning so he's going to meet us at the store around 1pm. I'll pick you up around 12pm."

Manipulator: "OK"

Target: "Hey Dad, you got all your tools?"

Manipulator: "I'm not going to get the door today. Me and my friend are going to come back on Tuesday..." 🚩 #3

Target: "Are you serious! Dad, why didn't you tell me that yesterday? Now I need to call my friend and stop him from coming with the truck! I drove 30 minutes in the opposite direction of my house just to come get you! I could have been over there painting all morning if you would have told me you weren't gonna hang the door!"

Manipulator: "Don't you want me to see the house?" 🚩 #4

Target: "I don't care if you see the house. My purpose in coming to get you was so we could get this door. I don't want to move in without the storm door because I don't want anybody to be able to just knock my front door down!"

Manipulator: "What? Yo' mama let you move into a bad neighborhood!" 🚩 #5

Target: "Of course not Dad. My house is in a great neighborhood. We had storm doors on all our

RED FLAG!

doors growing up and my mom has them on all her doors now. It would just make me feel safer."

RED FLAG EXPLANATIONS:

🚩 #1: "The lady brought me an iPad mini so I sent it back." What lady? Why is he depending on some lady to get the iPad? Why did he not just go to the store and buy one? She got the wrong one, he sent it back and just never got another iPad? I understand that people like to find "hook-ups". However, in this case it was likely an indication that he did not have the means to get what his daughter wanted in a typical manner. Especially since her birthday and Christmas are both in December and April had rolled around with no iPad.

🚩 #2: "Ok. Find the one you want and order it. We need somebody with a truck so we can pick it up." He is not going to give her the money for it and he does not have a way to pick it up either? He is making absolutely no effort to help. This decreases the chances greatly that he is going to get the door for her. If she orders it, she's responsible for paying for it. If she has to get someone with a truck, that person will be there to help her pick it up. Her dad basically just told her

"A storm door...that's a great idea. Go ahead and do that!" He has made a verbal commitment only with nothing concrete to back up that he is really going to do it.

🚩 #3: "I'm not going to get the door today. Me and my friend are going to come back on Tuesday..." Who is his friend and why would he want to bring someone to his daughter's home that she does not know? If he knew he needed until Tuesday, why would he waste her time today? This is inconsiderate. This father does not respect his daughter's time or privacy.

🚩 #4: "Don't you want me to see the house?" This is the start of shifting the blame and playing on her emotions. Because she is angry with him now he's going to play the victim. He wants her to feel bad for being angry when he only wanted to see the house. If all he wanted to do was see the house, he did not need to pretend like he was going to get the door. He could have just told the truth. He could have said he wouldn't be able to get the door until Tuesday but he would like to see where the house is and check everything out so everything would go smoothly when he came back. Instead, he manipulated her into coming to get him.

🚩 #5: "What? Yo' mama let you move into a bad

neighborhood!" When he could not make her feel bad he shifted the blame to someone else. Her mother was never even a part of the situation, yet he brought her into it and made her into a neglectful parent. In actuality, if he really cared that much he would have offered to check out the neighborhood and the house before she bought it. He is deflecting blame everywhere besides where it should be. With him. All he really needed to do was apologize for wasting her time. But, if he apologized that would mean he had done something wrong.

What is the manipulation? The father did not follow through on anything he said he would do for his daughter. Yet, he turns the entire scenario around and tries to make her feel guilty and make her mother look like the bad parent. He plays on his daughter's emotions to make himself seem like he was a caring father that wanted to see where his daughter lived. He was only concerned about himself. It didn't matter how she felt.

Why would a father manipulate his own daughter? He does not want to take responsibility. He does not want to look like the bad guy. He could have a deep sense of needing to feel special, important, etc. If he takes responsibility for anything it means he would have to admit his faults.

How does the daughter recognize and avoid being a target again? She must look at her father's history of behavior toward her. Obviously, this is not the first time he has disappointed her. She will need to change her expectation of him. She has to realize that while his behavior may or may not make him a bad a person, it certainly makes him an unreliable one. If you understand that your father is unreliable then you know you cannot count on him when you need him. You find others in your life that will replace the behavior that you are looking for from your father. You cannot replace your father because that's always who he will be. But, you do not continue to set yourself up to be disappointed by him. When you need someone to hang a door, you find a friend who loves doing handy work who will do it for you. You hire someone. You learn to do it yourself. You have several options to choose from, but you do not call your father. It will not likely take away the desire you have for your dad to be that person for you, but it will keep you from constant hurt and disappointment in that area.

RED FLAG!

Scenario #3:

Target: "Good morning Mom...how are you?

Manipulator: "Oh, I'm doing fine. I just came from having coffee with Margaret. You know she got a new dinning set."

Target: "Oh she did? Is it nice?"

Manipulator: "Yes it's nice. I sure would like to have a new kitchen table myself. But, I don't have the money for it." 🚩 #1

Target: "Really? You never sit at the table."

Manipulator: "Well, I would if I had a nice one like Margaret's. I'm ashamed to even invite anyone over. I'd get it too but you know I'm on a fixed income." 🚩 #2

Target: "I'll send you the money so you can get the table."

Manipulator: "I got the table but they coming to take it back!" 🚩 #3

Target: "What do you mean? I sent you more than enough money to pay for the table in full."

Manipulator: "Well, you know I didn't have nothing to eat and then your sister needed some money. If I don't pay them by the end of the week they coming to take it." #4

Target: "How much is it going to cost to pay it off?"

RED FLAG EXPLANATIONS:

#1: "I sure would like to have a new kitchen table myself. But, I don't have the money for it." The mother saying she would like to have something but not having the money is a guilt trip on the daughter. The mother knows the daughter has the money. She makes herself sound helpless because of her financial situation.

#2: "Well, I would if I had a nice one like Margaret's. I'm ashamed to even invite anyone over. I'd get it too but you know I'm on a fixed income." Telling the daughter that she feels ashamed to invite anyone over is an even bigger guilt trip. Now her mother is insinuating that she is lonely but does not have company because she is ashamed of what she does not have. Reiterating that she is on a fixed income is ensuring that her daughter knows that she has no opportunity to earn the money to help herself.

🚩 #3: "I got the table but they coming to take it back!" Who are THEY and why are they coming to take HER table? They would be the store she rented the table from instead of buying it so she could pocket or spend the money on something else. The panic and fear are not real. She could actually care less about the table. She wants her daughter to feel bad so she will send more money.

🚩 #4: "Well, you know I didn't have nothing to eat and then your sister needed some money. If I don't pay them by the end of the week they coming to take it." A good daughter would never want her mother to go hungry. Added guilt trip here. She even helped her sister too because she may have needed food as well. Any good mother wouldn't want her children to go hungry either. Now, because she needed food and she helped her other daughter who was in need as well, they are going to take her table. She needs that table or she'll be right back to where she was before. Alone, lonely and too ashamed to invite anyone over if her daughter does not send the money. The guilt trip will start all over again.

What is the manipulation? The mother feels like her daughter has money to spare and that she should have some. She never actually asks her daughter to buy the table. She just keeps bringing it up until the daughter offers. She uses guilt as her tactic to get money for what she wants. It may even sound legit if this was not the same tactic she used each time she wanted money.

Why would a mother manipulate her daughter in this way? Asking her daughter for something that's not a necessity may be responded to with a "no". However, if she could make her feel sorry for her, she is more likely to get it. Guilt is a powerful tool. A manipulator who uses this tactic does not care about how it effects the target. They really don't think about whether their actions are hurting anyone or not. They only care about getting what they want.

How does the daughter recognize and avoid being a target again? She has to first understand what makes her buy into this tactic. She cares about her mother and does not want her to go without. What she may need to do is to offer to purchase the item her mother wants instead of sending money. She may decide on a budget that she will allot for her mother and once that's gone it doesn't matter what she wants. She must understand that her mother is the kind of person who will manipulate to get what she wants. She needs to decide on her boundaries, set them and

RED FLAG!

stick to them. She will have to prepare herself for the consequences that will come with setting boundaries. Since her mother will be upset with her, she must be able to handle whatever that brings with it. Once you understand that you have a manipulative parent you can manage your life accordingly. It's not a reflection on you. Allowing yourself to be manipulated is not a part of honoring your mother. This is more about you and your guilt. You don't have to spend your life feeling guilty because of what someone else doesn't have. Eventually, you will give so much that you won't have anything left. Then where does that leave you? I'll answer that for you. It leaves you nowhere because you certainly cannot turn back to them if you need help.

The next section takes manipulation to the next level. We are now moving into abuse. Most cases of abuse either begin with or end with some type of manipulation. With many situations, the manipulation goes from start to finish and never ceases. Here is where it gets serious. We will now get into examples of physical, verbal, mental/emotional, sexual and spiritual abuse. The last subsection of abuse differs from the first five in that it is meant to shed light on how we can cause harm to ourselves. If the Red Flag! is not acted upon, there is often damage that lasts for years and even goes through generations.

RED FLAG!

Section #2: Abuse

What is abuse? The first two definitions found in the Merriam-Webster dictionary are

1: a corrupt practice or custom
2: improper or excessive use or treatment

Who might experience abuse? Anyone can be a victim of abuse. However, abusive incidences of women and children are more often reported.

Why are certain people chosen as targets? Abusers often have a "type" they go after. The target is typically something or someone they like. However, there are some who have targets of convenience. No one is exempt. If what they like is not available, it could also be whatever is more easily accessible.

Characteristics of an Abuser: When you want to spot an abuser do not focus on his or her physical appearance. There is no set look. What you want to pay attention to are behaviors. However, they are often very likable individuals. They have to be or no one would be drawn to them. Abusers are typically individuals who seek to isolate and control you in order to meet a need or desire they have. It may seem overprotective and caring at first. You may see two different people. Meaning, they are one way in public and the complete opposite behind closed doors. You may always be on eggshells because of an explosive temper that can be set off by almost anything and often nothing. You might hear threats on a regular basis either to harm you or someone you love. This is a tactic to keep you scared silent.

How does one escape an abuser? Very carefully. You need a support system and a plan. If at all possible, do not do this on your own. It will depend on what type of abuse you're experiencing, but it will take a village. If you have trustworthy friends and family, keep them informed. If not, there are hotlines, shelters, counselors and other authorities that can help. The first thing that has to happen is that you recognize you're being abused and you admit it. Check out www.thehotline.org or call 1-800-799-7233.

RED FLAG!

Subsection A: Physical Abuse
Scenario #1

Perpetrator: Silently walks past his target because he is upset with her from a disagreement they had earlier. 🚩 #1

Target: Feels the tension in the house so she walks by silently and goes to sit down to call her sister.

Perpetrator: Hears her on the phone, comes into the room where she is and demands that she hang up. He mouths it silently, with hand gestures so whoever she's talking to can't hear. 🚩 #2

Target: Hangs up the phone and comes toward the perpetrator thinking he wanted her to hang up so they could talk.

Perpetrator: While approaching each other in the hallway, she begins to speak and he lunges at her. She jumps back into the wall and he laughs. 🚩 #3

Target: Now visibly afraid and confused, she tries to stay out of his way without making eye contact.

Perpetrator: The next time he passes her, he lunges again. But, this time it's with his fist. 🚩 #4

RED FLAG EXPLANATIONS:

🚩 #1: Silently walks past his target because he is upset with her from a disagreement they had earlier: The silent treatment can be used as a passive aggressive show of force. Not winning the previous argument is a sign of weakness for the perpetrator. Weakness is not an option. He believes he should always win. Of course, this is building unhealthy tension.

🚩 #2: Hears her on the phone, comes into the room where she is and demands that she hang up. He mouths it silently, with hand gestures so whoever she's talking to can't hear: Isolation is key for this perpetrator. There can be no witnesses to what happens so it will be his word against hers. Without isolation he does not have complete control. He does not want her on the phone, but no one needs to be able to hear him or see him get angry with her. He needs to be seen as the good guy so people are confused by her story should she ever tell it. If he yells at her in the presence of others it may portray him as a mean person.

🚩 #3: While approaching each other in the hallway, she begins to speak and he lunges at her. She jumps back into the wall and he laughs: This is the first show of physical force. He needs to instill fear in her and he wants to see that she is afraid of him. This makes him feel he's in control and that he can and will win. His tension is building and his anger is growing but he has no outlet as of yet. He has just shown her that he has absolutely no respect for her as a partner. Fear is about control...not love.

#4: The next time he passes her, he lunges again. But, this time it's with his fist: This is the point of no return. Rest assured that if he'll hit her once he will do it again. However, he is ok now. Things can go back to normal because he has gotten his release. She is once again beneath him. He has regained control. He has won the disagreement. His shame is gone and he has no guilt about what he has done. Sure, he may cry, bring flowers, make her dinner and tell her that he's sorry and that he loves her. Those types of things will likely only take place if she tries to leave. However, the truth is, in his mind he now owns her.

What is the abuse? This abuse is both mental and physical. The perpetrator has figured out that he can scare his girlfriend into submission and it makes him feel good. The scare tactic was the mental part of the abuse. Of course, the lunge with the fist was the physical. He knew she was afraid of him because she had already flinched hard enough to hit the wall and that amused him. He just took it a step farther to ensure she knew that she should not challenge him again.

Why would a boyfriend treat his girlfriend this way? The perpetrator does not know how to effectively cope with his insecurities. He becomes emotional but does not want to show weakness, so he resorts to what makes him feel strong. He may have seen this behavior growing up or may have picked it up from past relationships where it worked for him. It's really not her job to figure out why he is the way he is. At this point, it's time for her to figure out how she plans to protect herself.

How do you recognize and avoid a situation like this? She must first realize that she is in an abusive relationship. It will be easy to say "it only happened once." It does not matter how many times it's happened. What matters is that it did. If he will lunge at you he will hit you. If he will do it once he will do it again. These are just things that you have to know. If you see the behavior, believe it. No matter what he says. No matter what sob story he may give you about his reason for doing it. He needs help and so do you. We all have a past, but nothing gives anyone the right to abuse you. It is possible, but you will not likely be able to remain with him while he works through his issues should he decide to get help. You need to

RED FLAG!

plan your exodus immediately. Even if you do not leave right away, you need to know what it will look like if you make that decision. You must do this carefully. You need a team. Do not try to do this alone. You need to have a safety plan that includes friends and family that believe you, a place to escape to, legal involvement and money. You may also have to change up everything you're used to doing. Again, you will need help to accomplish this.

RED FLAG!

Scenario #2

Target: After being beaten up she decided to leave. 🚩 #1

Perpetrator: He came by her mother's house with some food and money. He told her mother and grandmother he loved her and their kids and he wanted her to come back. 🚩 #2

Target: Being talked into it by her family, she returned. 🚩 #3

Perpetrator: "You thought you could get away from me?" 🚩 #4

Target: "You got a whole other girl and kids. Why you need me?"

Perpetrator: "I don't need you but you mine." He beat her again that night. 🚩 #5

Target: Waited until he left for work, packed up her kids and went back to her mother's house.

Perpetrator: Called her on the phone to say "Evidently you don't remember what I told you!" 🚩 #6

Target: "I just want you to leave me alone."

Perpetrator: "You gon' die today!"  #7

RED FLAG EXPLANATIONS:

🚩 **#1:** After being beaten up she decided to leave: If he has already beaten her up once, chances are it will happen again. She made the right decision to leave but she needed a complete safety plan. Leaving immediately gave her a good chance of survival. However, not having enough assistance may have left her open

🚩 **#2:** He came by her mother's house with some food and money. He told her mother and grandmother he loved her and their kids and he wanted her to come back: It is typical for the perpetrator to attempt to make up with you, especially in front of others. This gives the impression that he really is a good guy and that maybe you deserved what happened. Or maybe, there was just a misunderstanding that you overreacted to.

🚩 **#3:** Being talked into it by her family, she returned: There is a huge issue within this girl's family. They respond to money above anything

RED FLAG!

else so they believe everything he says when he shows up offering financial apologies. If your family cares more about money than they do about you, then they are not a good safety plan. They are a part of the problem. You will need to look for assistance outside of your family. But, just because they send you back into the lion's den doesn't mean you should go. Some of you will need a safety Plan B.

🚩 #4: "You thought you could get away from me?" Now she realizes that the apology he gave wasn't as sincere as she may have thought. It's certainly not what her family thought it was. It's possible that she is now in a life or death situation with her children. She originally got away from him, but she returned. He has just proven to her that he is all she has and that he has her family in his pocket.

🚩 #5: "I don't need you but you mine." If she belongs to him then it means he can do anything he wants to her. He doesn't necessarily want or need her in his life but he will keep her because she is a possession. Think about it. He just purchased her back from her own family. She is more like property now rather than a person.

🚩 #6: "Evidently you don't remember what I told you!" When a perpetrator makes a threat, no matter how outrageous it might sound, believe him. The police may or may not take him into custody if you call. You should be documenting behavior and phone calls. You should have already been in contact with a domestic violence counselor by now. If you haven't done it, do it now! Do not go back to your family. It will make you and them sitting ducks.

🚩 **#7:** "You gon' die today!" This is the ultimate threat and he is not making it just to hear himself talk. He means this. At this point, you and your children should be nowhere to be found. Your family should be on high alert and the police should already be involved.

What is the abuse? This is physical abuse mixed with verbal and mental abuse. This is an abuser who is willing to progress through the process unto death if he feels it's necessary. If he gets the notion in his head that "if I can't have you no one will..." it means he will not stop.

Why would a boyfriend treat his girlfriend this way? This perpetrator is all about image. He has a pretty young girl that he has control over. He has more money than her family and that's appealing to them. He knows this. When his money stops impressing her, he has to find another way to keep her. Now, the once nice guy that treated her

RED FLAG!

so well has to use fear.

How do you recognize and avoid a situation like this? She must realize that she does not have any support. She is in a relationship with a man who does not respect her and her family is of no help. She has to find someone that will believe what is happening to her and has the power to assist her. Never give any one person all of your power. You must always have a way that you can survive without them. There were likely many Red Flags before the first punch was thrown. It typically begins with verbal abuse to diminish your confidence and self-esteem. Then it progresses into mental abuse. You begin to feel worthless and helpless because of the things he's saying to you. Once your defenses are down, you don't even see the punches coming. Always have someone who is for you and knows what you are really dealing with. Do not lie to your friends about what's going on. If no one can see you then no one can rescue you. Do not allow yourself to be completely isolated from the life you had before you met him. Get help!

RED FLAG!

Scenario #3

Target: Sat on the sofa as the children ran by playing loudly.

Perpetrator: Screamed at the children and then yelled at her for not making them get quiet. 🚩 #1

Target: Noticed a beer in his hand and understood that she needed to act quickly. 🚩 #2

Perpetrator: Jumped up and let his fist connect with her face as she ran toward the children. 🚩 #3

Target: Picked herself up off the floor and ran to lock herself in her bedroom with the children.

Perpetrator: Fell asleep in his chair in a drunken haze. He awoke the next morning to find his wife and children gone. He found them quickly because the only place she could go was to her mother's.

Target: Sat in her old bedroom at her mother's home contemplating her next move.

Perpetrator: Shows up at the mother's home begging, pleading and crying for his wife to return. He assured her that he was sorry and that it would never happen again. 🚩 #4

Target: Wanted so badly to believe his tears and his apology that she went against her better judgement and went with her feelings. She returned home with him. 🚩 #5

Perpetrator: As soon as his wife walked through the door, he locked the children in the bedroom and beat his wife until the blood and tears that ran down her face soon ran down his hands. 🚩 #6

Target: Begged her husband to let her live. 🚩 #7

Perpetrator: Laughed and told her that even if she lived no one would want her. 🚩 #8

RED FLAG EXPLANATIONS:

🚩 **#1:** Screamed at the children and then yelled at her for not making them get quiet: Losing his temper and yelling at the kids to be quiet is not necessarily a horrible thing. The issue is that in this scenario, the perpetrator is blaming the target for not making the kids be quiet. Not only has he made it her fault the kids are loud, but he expected her to read his mind. From now on, she and the kids will walk on eggshells because she is

RED FLAG!

expected to know what he wants without him saying it.

#2: Noticed a beer in his hand and understood that she needed to act quickly: If noticing a beer in his hand lets her know she should move quickly, this likely indicates he has a drinking problem. If his personality completely changes because there's a beer in his hand, he needs help. The issue is that she cannot be the one to help him. If she says anything it will cause her more problems.

#3: Jumped up and let his fist connect with her face as she ran toward the children: This target cannot win. She was in the process of doing what he asked her to, but she still got hit. If you find yourself in a situation where you can't win no matter what you do, it's time for you to get out of that situation.

#4: Shows up at the mother's home begging, pleading and crying for his wife to return. He assured her that he was sorry and that it would never happen again: This is typical of an abuser the first time he is left. They have a sad, sob story. It's highly believable and it may even be true for them. There are often tears and certainly apologies, but it does not mean what the target thinks it means. It's never an accident when someone's fist slams into your face or any other part of your body for that matter. There are some things that happen where an apology after the fact just doesn't cut it. This is one of those times.

🚩 **#5:** Wanted so badly to believe his tears and his apology that she went against her better judgement and went with her feelings. She returned home with him: If you know you are going against your better judgement... don't! This is your gut and instincts warning you and you are ignoring it.

🚩 **#6:** As soon as his wife walked through the door, he locked the children in the bedroom and beat his wife until the blood and tears that ran down her face soon ran down his hands: She's trapped! He knows she's not going anywhere without her kids. The next time the abuse happens it will be worse. It will continue to get progressively worse...if she survives. This will happen unless he gets help.

🚩 **#7:** Begged her husband to let her live: Having to beg for her life means he is no longer looking at her as a person he once loved. Her thoughts, feelings and desires do not matter to him. She must not forget that, in his mind, she deserves to be treated like this because she humiliated him. She made him look like a fool in

RED FLAG!

front of her mother when he had to beg for her to open the door. Now, she's paying for what she did to him because he never did anything wrong. In his mind, she deserves what she gets because this whole thing was her fault.

#8: Laughed and told her that even if she lived no one would want her: He's laughing at her which means he is thoroughly enjoying this. If she makes it he's trying to ensure that she's unrecognizable. This has gone into being sadistic. He no longer has feelings either. He is consumed by power. The more she cries and begs the stronger he gets. This must now turn into a mind game on her part. If she knows of anything that will make him stop she has to think of it and do it immediately. If not, this may be one of those times where playing dead or unconscious may work because that's what he wants. Do whatever you have to do to live.

What is the abuse? This is physical abuse possibly induced by alcohol abuse. He may be a different person sober, but the alcohol tends to bring out the person being suppressed when sober. It's possible that he is only abusive when he's drinking. However, that's still a problem because apparently, he drinks regularly. This may be a person who could change his behavior if he became sober. The issue is that he has to want it for himself.

Why would a husband treat his wife and kids this way? Drinking is how he copes with his issues instead of handling them appropriately. Using alcohol is a negative coping mechanism. It makes him feel slightly better because he can temporarily escape the problems he cannot figure out how to deal with. However, it adds problems for the target. In his drunken state, he does not care about anything or anyone. If someone could get through to him to get help, things may get better. Unfortunately, his wife will not be the one to get through to him.

How do you recognize and avoid a situation like this? Of course, she already recognized that he had a problem with drinking. She also knew that his drinking made him violent toward her. It may be a good idea to try and make friends with the neighbors or have family and friends on standby. There needs to be someone who she and the kids can get to quickly. Take note of when he is drinking. Once he has grabbed that first beer out of the fridge she has to take action. If you get out of the house once, do not go back. Resist his crying and pleading. Get a restraining order. Contact a domestic violence shelter for assistance because even though you may be safe for the moment with your mother, you need a plan.

RED FLAG!

Understand that he is sick and needs help. He cannot do it on his own and you can't help him. Your responsibility is to yourself and your children. He must decide for himself that he wants to get help. Once you are in a life and death situation with him in control, there isn't much you can do. Do not ignore what your gut is telling you. It's usually trying to inform and protect you.

SONEAKQUA J. WHITE

RED FLAG!

Subsection B: Verbal Abuse
Scenario #1

Perpetrator: "Hey Stupid! Where are you? Get in here!" 🚩 #1

Target: "I'm right here." 🚩 #2

Perpetrator: "You know...to be so smart you sure are stupid!" 🚩 #3

Target: "What did I do?"

Perpetrator: "Nothing. You just look stupid. We shouldn't have had a third kid because the first two were dumb enough. Then you came along." 🚩 #4

Target: "Can I go now?"

Perpetrator: "No! You stand right there until we finish this conversation! Then you can take your stupid self in the kitchen and get me a glass of water."

Target: "I need to go study so maybe I won't be stupid anymore." 🚩 #5

Perpetrator: "You can study but you'll still be stupid. Maybe you can find somebody dumb enough to marry you because you sure won't be able to take care of yourself." 🚩 #6

RED FLAG EXPLANATIONS:

🚩 #1: "Hey Stupid! Where are you? Get in here!" If referring to a child as "Stupid" is not a Red Flag! I don't know what is. A mother is the first person who shows a child how to love and be loved. A father is the first person who shows a child how to protect themselves or to be protected. Feeling loved and safe are necessities. If her own parent thinks she's stupid, how will she learn to cope with how the rest of the world views her? How will she view herself?

🚩 #2: "I'm right here." This child is answering to being called "Stupid" by her parent as if it is her name. Of course, she knows it's not her name, but she is beginning to identify with it. Each time she is called this it is becoming more and more of her identity. Until one day she does not recognize who she really is. She will deny being smart, beautiful or capable no matter who tells her she is or how many times they tell her. Her self-esteem will be non-existent. That is, unless she is one of those kids who can force themselves to be the opposite

RED FLAG!

of what the parent says they are.

🚩 #3: "You know...to be so smart you sure are stupid!" Using smart and stupid in the same sentence being directed toward her is confusing. Which is it? Is she smart or stupid? Typically, we pick up on what is being repeated or the last thing being said. The smart part will be negated and deleted. Only stupid will remain.

🚩 #4: "Nothing. You just look stupid. We shouldn't have had a third kid because the first two were dumb enough. Then you came along." Now, not only has this parent insulted the child's intelligence, but has also downgraded the way she looks. This child is being destroyed from the inside out. She has also been compared to her two older siblings deeming her the worst. Was she put on earth or born into this family just to suffer?

🚩 #5: "I need to go study so maybe I won't be stupid anymore." She has bought into the idea of being stupid, yet she is still young enough to believe she can do something about it. If she studies, she might be able to improve. The problem here is that she is trying to impress and gain approval of the parent, which she will not obtain. This child now believes that the way she is being treated is her fault and that she can make it better. Unfortunately, there is nothing she can do to make this better because it's not really about her.

🚩 **#6:** "You can study but you'll still be stupid. Maybe you can find somebody dumb enough to marry you because you sure won't be able to take care of yourself." The parent is now working on killing the dreams of this child. She had hopes that if she studied she could improve. Now, she's being told that her only chance is to find someone who would settle for marrying her. He would have to be pretty dumb to do it but maybe somehow she could pull it off. She'll never get any smarter and won't even be able to get a job. Forget college. Just trap the first guy she meets into marrying her before he finds out how stupid she really is.

What is the abuse? This is verbal abuse that has lasting mental and emotional effects attached to it. This is a child who could have every chance in the world to thrive, but she has a parent who will not allow it. He has not yet laid a hand on her but he doesn't have to. The words he's using are beating her to a pulp.

Why would a parent treat a child this way? You've heard it before. Hurt people, hurt people. There is absolutely nothing wrong with this child. However, there is something wrong with this parent. Typically, abusers hurt people to make

RED FLAG!

themselves feel better. Even if it doesn't make them feel better, at least someone else is feeling as much pain or more than they are. A child is an easy target. They are accessible and eager to please.

How do you recognize and avoid a situation like this? Despite what this parent would have her to believe she must be able to see the truth. She can give herself goals that she can accomplish on her own. Remind herself that she can be good to herself even if no one else is. No one deserves to be talked down to. Whenever something is said or done that makes you feel bad, you must evaluate. Ask yourself if what they're saying is a fact and if it can be changed. A child does not have the best coping skills so there needs to be someone they trust who can help them cope until they can get out of the situation. Teach your children and yourself how to self-talk. Instead of removing the negative, completely reframe. For example, instead of saying "I'm not stupid..." say "I am brilliant, I am capable and I am successful!" Affirm yourself in the positive instead of simply trying to deny the negative.

RED FLAG!

Scenario #2

Perpetrator: "So, what are you planning to do after you graduate high school?"

Target: "I want to go to college with my sister."

Perpetrator: "Boy! Your sister got a different daddy and she got a scholarship!" 🚩 #1

Target: "What does that have to do with anything?"

Perpetrator: "You just like you no good daddy and ain't nobody paying for you to go to school." 🚩 #2

Target: "So, I'm not good enough?"

Perpetrator: "Naw. You ain't gon' never be as a good as your sister." 🚩 #3

Target: "I'm not trying to be her. But, why is she good enough to go to school and not me?"

Perpetrator: "You can't be her. And shut up! I'm talking!" 🚩 #4

Target: "You can't help me like you helped her?"

Perpetrator: "Please…I'm not about to waste no money on somebody who gon' flunk out."
🚩 #5

Target: "I'm making straight A's right now. Why do you think I'm gonna flunk out?"

Perpetrator: "You act like you ain't cheating."
🚩 #6

Target: "You think I have to cheat? You don't think I'm smart enough to do my own work and pass?"

Perpetrator: "Naw! Your daddy cheated all the time and everybody thought he was smart."
🚩 #7

RED FLAG EXPLANATIONS:

🚩 **#1:** "Boy! Your sister got a different daddy and she got a scholarship!" What does having a different father have to do with this child going to college? How is it his fault that his mother had children by different fathers? Making differences between children causes more issues than people might think. Did she forget that she chose his father to sleep with? Why is the child treated differently because of his father?

RED FLAG!

🚩 **#2:** "You just like you no good daddy and ain't nobody paying for you to go to school." This boy has been labeled "no good" by his own family because of something outside of his control. He didn't choose his father. Yet, he's being told that simply because of who his father is it makes him unworthy. He's not being measured for who is. He's being treated a certain way based off someone else's decisions.

🚩 **#3:** "Naw. You ain't gon' never be as a good as your sister." He'll never measure up to his sister. This is the type of talk that pits siblings against one another. This child now knows that he is not loved the same as his sister and it sounds as if he's not even liked by his family. This boy, who may have never had an issue with his sister, may feel differently about her after this conversation.

🚩 **#4:** "You can't be her. And shut up! I'm talking!" This further seals the message that the family wants to get into his head. There is absolutely nothing he can ever do to measure up to his sister. Self-esteem is affected by these words. Now, he can't speak. He couldn't possibly win a case that's already stacked against him. He never got a chance and it looks like he never will with his family.

🚩 **#5:** "Please...I'm not about to waste no

money on somebody who gon' flunk out." Before he even gets the opportunity, he's being told that he will flunk out. Not just fail a test or a paper. He's going to have such an epic fail that the school will kick him out! Coming from family, this is detrimental. Who will believe in him if his own family doesn't? Will he and can he continue to believe in himself when everyone around him is almost planning for him to fail? It's difficult but possible.

🚩 #6: "You act like you ain't cheating." On top of everything else, they think he has cheated his way through high school because he couldn't possibly be smart enough to pass on his own. To find out that this is what his family has always thought of him is devastating. Have they been paying attention at all? If they thought he was cheating, they could simply have had him get a book out and ask him some questions. Instead of doing any research, they just assumed. They think nothing of him.

🚩 #7: "Naw! Your daddy cheated all the time and everybody thought he was smart." Here it is again. He is being punished because of a man they chose, whom he does not know. Sure, DNA does have an impact on physical and behavioral traits. However, doesn't everyone deserve a chance to show who they are? Everyone just wants to be

RED FLAG!

loved and accepted for who they are and this child did not have that opportunity. He is being judged for traits he has nothing to do with.

What is the abuse? This is verbal abuse that if accepted will have lasting mental and emotional side effects. This boy is being shown that he doesn't have a chance in the world of being himself if he remains around his family. He is not being seen or heard. He's being judged. Being compared to his sister, whom he will never measure up to in their eyes, is unfair.

Why would a parent treat a child this way? This parent is angry with this child's father and since the father is not around, the pain is heaped onto his son. This is heartbreaking but it happens daily. This parent wants someone to be punished and to feel pain like she does. The boy is her scapegoat. Maybe he looks like his father. Maybe he even walks, talks and sounds like him. It still doesn't make them the same person.

How do you recognize and avoid a situation like this? This child must realize that this is not about him. They do not even see him. If he cannot escape physically he can escape mentally. He needs absolute determination. He must get out of this environment in order to thrive. Otherwise, he may actually start to believe what they are saying.

There must be others around him who can speak life into him instead of the death that he is currently listening to. His sister may be able to help. A school counselor, teacher or coach are great options. He will need to speak life to himself daily as well. "I can and I will go to college. I am not my father. I am me and I am enough." It is often difficult for a young person to disconnect from their family. However, there are times when it's necessary. Join a team at school. Get involved in a ministry. Align yourself with people who can be a positive influence in your life. It only takes one person to make a difference.

RED FLAG!

Scenario #3

Perpetrator: "I don't want you talking to your cousin anymore." 🚩 #1

Target: "Why? She's my best friend."

Perpetrator: "Exactly! She puts dumb ideas in your head and you're already dumb enough." 🚩 #2

Target: "I have a mind of my own. She doesn't make me do anything I don't want to do."

Perpetrator: "I don't like her and I don't want her around. End of conversation."

Target: "You can't tell me who I can and cannot talk to."

Perpetrator: "Yes I can. If you don't want a black eye you'll do what I tell you." 🚩 #3

Target: "Oh now you're gonna hit me?"

Perpetrator: "Only if I have to. If you make me do it. It'll be your fault." 🚩 #4

Target: "Then I guess it's time for me to leave this relationship."

Perpetrator: "Where you gonna go? You don't have money, no friends and you got two kids. Nobody's gonna want you now!" #5

Target: "I'll get a job."

Perpetrator: "Nobody's gonna hire you. You haven't worked in years and you have no skills! I only got with you because you were pretty and you don't even have that anymore!" #6

RED FLAG EXPLANATIONS:

#1: "I don't want you talking to your cousin anymore." This is control. Be leery of anyone who tries to keep you away from your family. This is a setup. If no one can see you no one can find out what's happening to you. Never allow yourself to be put into a position where you have no one to talk to.

#2: "Exactly! She puts dumb ideas in your head and you're already dumb enough." Her self-esteem is being attacked by him calling her dumb. He's also calling her cousin dumb and insinuating that his wife cannot think for herself. This is also a sign of him letting her know that he wants to be

RED FLAG!

the only one she listens to. He cannot have absolute control if there are outside sources that she trusts.

🚩 **#3:** "Yes I can. If you don't want a black eye you'll do what I tell you." Abusers do not like to be challenged. If she will not comply by verbal force then physical force may be imminent. If she hasn't realized at this point that she needs to get out of the relationship, she should know right now. Do not take the verbal threat of physical violence lightly.

🚩 **#4:** "Only if I have to. If you make me do it. It'll be your fault." This is a warning. Even if he doesn't hit her in this moment, it is only a matter of time. He is telling her that if she does not comply with his warning he will have to hit her to make her comply. In his eyes, that's what will make it her fault. In other words, all she has to do is what he says and nothing further has to take place. However, if she doesn't do what he says, then she's making the choice to be hit.

🚩 **#5:** "Where you gonna go? You don't have money, no friends and you got two kids. Nobody's gonna want you now!" He is telling her that she's trapped. She needs him. No one else will want her because she's damaged or of no use to anyone else. This was likely what he set up so that if the day ever arose that she wanted to leave, she would be in this position. This is a warning to all stay-at-home parents. You need to have something set up in case your spouse ever tries to pull this on you. You never want to completely depend on any one person for everything.

🚩 **#6:** "Nobody's gonna hire you. You haven't worked in years and you have no skills! I only got with you because you were pretty and you don't even have that anymore!" This is again to attack her self-esteem. If she wasn't already down, here's the sucker punch. There is always some truth wrapped in the lie so that it is believable. She hasn't worked outside the home in years, but she shouldn't think for one moment that she has no skills. She is still the same person she was before she met him. It may be buried but she needs to find it.

What is the abuse? This is verbal abuse with the intent to damage mentally. It also has the potential to escalate to physical abuse. This perpetrator wants to control the target. The verbal assault is meant to weaken and break her spirit so he won't have to hit her. But, if it doesn't work like he hopes, then he has to let her know that he will take further action.

Why would a spouse treat another spouse this

RED FLAG!

way? Control is maddening. It makes some people feel invincible to have power and control over another person. You will see this in relationships as well as the workplace. The perpetrator here wants to be the only one the target listens to. He is threatened by anything and anyone else. In order to show himself strong, he needs to make sure she is weakened.

How do you recognize and avoid a situation like this? Realize that this situation will not get any better without help. The perpetrator is escalating because he is not getting the desired outcome he is looking for. If you do not want to lose yourself in a relationship like this and possibly become a physically battered woman, you need to plan for how to get help and how to keep yourself safe in the meantime. He is already starting to try and isolate you from the people you're closest to. It's only a matter of time before he has instilled so much fear in you that you will comply with whatever he says so as not to escalate the situation. Do not stop talking to your cousin. You might need her to help you get out. You're just going to have to do it without him knowing about it. This is where you need to be innovative. If you've been a stay-at-home parent, then you have all the qualifications of a caretaker. Find a resume of a nanny or in-home nurse and match your skills to theirs. Find a place to go and start applying for jobs. Do not allow yourself to solely depend on him any longer. Have a safety plan on hand so that if nothing gets better you know how you will get out.

RED FLAG!

Subsection C: Mental/Emotional Abuse
Scenario #1

Perpetrator: "I really need you to come through for me tonight and not leave me hanging at the last minute." 🚩 #1

Target: "I don't want to do it because I won't be able to face myself in the morning."

Perpetrator: "I understand. But, if you do it, it would mean that you love me sooo much and I'd owe you big time!" 🚩 #2

Target: "But, I'm nervous and I feel like this is all I'm good for."

Perpetrator: "It's gon' be ok. I'ma be right there with you the whole time."

Target: "Fine. I'ma do this for you but don't ask me again."

Perpetrator: "Well, you can't stop me from asking. You always have the right to say no." 🚩 #3

RED FLAG EXPLANATIONS:

🚩 **#1:** "I really need you to come through for me tonight and not leave me hanging at the last minute." This is guilt 101! The perpetrator in this scenario wants something from the target and is trying to make her feel guilty about not doing it. She is making it seem as if there is no one else that can do it. This is a tactic to put the responsibility on the target when it's really not her problem. Not only is she being convinced she's the only one who can do it, but she wasn't given enough time to try and get someone else. Guilt and shame condemn people. No one wants to feel this way, so most will do anything possible to get rid of those feelings.

🚩 **#2:** "I understand. But, if you do it, it would mean that you love me sooo much and I'd owe you big time!" So what you're saying is...if I don't do it then I don't love you. It doesn't matter how I feel about it. I just told you that I won't be able to look at myself in the morning and your reply is basically that I'll do it anyway if I love you. Putting the desires of others before your own needs is the fastest way to lose yourself. Hurting yourself to make someone else happy will end in disaster for you. If they don't care how what they do affects you, you have the right to protect yourself.

RED FLAG!

#3: "Well, you can't stop me from asking. You always have the right to say no." Yes, you do have the right to say no. But, catch what is being said. You cannot stop her from asking so you will be asked to compromise yourself again. While you do have the right to say no, what you're being told is that if I got you to do it this time, I will get you to do it again. In this instance, you do not need to explain your feelings again because she does not care. Let the word "no" be a complete sentence. It needs no explanation. Do not compromise your health physically, mentally, emotionally, spiritually or sexually to accommodate someone else's desires.

What is the abuse? This is mental/emotional abuse. The perpetrator has guilted the target into doing something she does not want to do. She has made her feel that if she doesn't do it then it means she does not love her. The target has now been made responsible for the perpetrator's feelings. So, now not only is she letting her down, but she doesn't love her either.

Why would a friend treat another friend like this? Be careful who you call a friend and why you befriend them. Manipulative and abusive people look for your weaknesses. This target happens to be a young woman who is just looking for someone to love her and she falls in love with anyone she thinks loves her back. The manipulator knows this information and she uses it against her. Emotional/Mental manipulation and abuse are just the beginning. Getting inside someone's head and learning how to tap into their emotions are the first steps to control. If I know what makes you tick...I can control your clock.

How do you recognize or avoid a situation like this? This type of manipulation is not always easy to recognize. People want to feel useful, needed and loved. However, maybe this girl didn't really know what love was. In that case, she fell for what she thought it was. Get away from a person who makes you feel bad without any regard for how you feel. You need help to do this because you may not be strong enough to stand up for yourself yet. You cannot be afraid to tell someone that you are in a situation that you need to escape from. You need an accountability partner who knows what's going on and will not judge you. This may sound easy to walk away from but it's not. When someone has convinced your mind that what they want is more important than what you need, you are in trouble. When you have been convinced that love hurts, it's difficult to believe that you should leave. You may need someone who is on the outside looking in to take you by the hand and walk you out.

RED FLAG!

Scenario #2

Target: "I think I want chicken wings with ranch dressing and French fries!"

Perpetrator: "Waiter...she'll have a salad with a light dressing on the side. I'll have the wings and fries." 🚩 #1

Target: "Why did you do that? I can eat whatever I want."

Perpetrator: "You can't eat whatever you want and be with me. You're getting fat and I don't like it." 🚩 #2

Target: "I weigh the same now as when I met you."

Perpetrator: "The scale must be wrong because you are definitely getting fat!" 🚩 #3

Target: "So, you're saying you're gonna break up with me if I gain weight?" 🚩 #4

Perpetrator: "No. I'm not gonna break up with you but I am gonna cheat on you. Nobody will want you anyway because you're fat." 🚩 #5

Target: "What are you talking about? We might as

well just break up now."

Perpetrator: "We break up when I say we break up. Just shut up and eat your stupid salad!" 🚩 #6

RED FLAG EXPLANATIONS:

🚩 #1: "Waiter…she'll have a salad with a light dressing on the side. I'll have the wings and fries." This is really a double Red Flag! He cancels and changes her order and then he orders what she wanted for himself to eat. He's not going to allow her to have what she wants but he's also going to torture her by eating what she wanted in front of her.

🚩 #2: "You can't eat whatever you want and be with me. You're getting fat and I don't like it." Another double Red Flag. Now, in order to be with him she has to eat what he tells her to eat. He doesn't like the way she looks so he's going to take control of her nutrition. If she's ever wondered what feeling powerless is like she's about to find out.

🚩 #3: "The scale must be wrong because you are definitely getting fat!" This is meant to make

RED FLAG!

her second guess herself. She's saying that there's been no change in her weight because she's monitoring it herself. However, he's telling her she's wrong. No matter what she believes, whatever he thinks overrides what she thinks and how she feels.

#4: "So, you're saying you're gonna break up with me if I gain weight?" She's missing the point. It doesn't matter whether or not he'll break up with her for gaining weight. The point is that he is taking control over her. He's putting her under a microscope that she doesn't have the lens into. She cannot see what he's talking about with the weight gain probably because it doesn't exist. What she doesn't realize is that she's walking into a situation where there is no way for her to win. If she remains in the relationship this will only get worse. She will no longer be her own person who is able to make her own decisions.

#5: "No. I'm not gonna break up with you but I am gonna cheat on you. Nobody will want you anyway because you're fat." Believe what he's saying. If she stays, he will feel like he has the right to cheat on her. He is working on beating her self-esteem so far into the ground that she will believe that he's the only one who will love her. Calling her fat is just the beginning. Right now, she's not buying into what he's saying but it's only a matter a time before she starts to agree with him.

🚩 **#6:** "We break up when I say we break up. Just shut up and eat your stupid salad!"

WARNING! If she hadn't realized that she needed to escape the relationship before, she should know it now. He is escalating. He's telling her that she doesn't have the right to leave the relationship. He just told her that he is in complete control. Now, she needs help to get out because she has become his possession. She no longer has the right to speak unless he gives her permission. If it hasn't already, this will likely lead to physical abuse.

What is the abuse? This is mental/emotional abuse. This is how it can begin. At first, it may be subtle. It may even appear that he's saying or doing something for her own good. But, it can escalate very quickly without her noticing when it switched from helpful to harmful.

Why would a boyfriend treat his girlfriend this way? There are many reasons why this behavior takes place. Abusers like to be in control. They thrive off of it. Many of them also thrive off of your fear because it makes them feel powerful.

How do you recognize and avoid a situation like this? Understand that everyone has rights. This

RED FLAG!

abusive situation has threatened to take away this young lady's basic right to eat what she wants. She is no longer in control of her own body in this scenario. She is being told something that contradicts her beliefs about herself while being forced to act as if it is a fact. Be leery of anyone who tries to control you with words or force. Do not let anyone be the only source you have to fact check against. Remember that "fat" can be subjective. If you like the way you look that's all that matters. Get away from anyone who threatens to shake your confidence in who you are. You should be able to take a criticism or leave it. If someone is trying to force you to see their way as the only way, there's a problem. We all have choices. If ever you feel like you don't have a choice, your choice should be one of escape.

RED FLAG!

Scenario #3

Perpetrator: "Are you a new in-home specialist?"

Target: "No. I'm the new inhouse therapist."

Perpetrator: "Oh. You're an intern. Who's supervising you?" 🚩#1

Target: "I'm not an intern. I'm fully licensed."

Perpetrator: "You're fully licensed?" 🚩#2

Target: "Yes".

Perpetrator: "You...are fully licensed." 🚩#3

Target: "Yes."

Perpetrator: "Oh! Well you should take over the juvenile justice kids. You should be really good with them." 🚩#4

RED FLAG EXPLANATIONS:

🚩 **#1:** "Oh. You're an intern. Who's supervising you?" First, you guess that I'm a home specialist.

Anyone can take a chance and get it wrong. But, you could have simply asked instead of assuming. You've already guessed at my position once and were corrected. Now, you've been told what my position is, and you assume again that I am ranked lower than what I'm telling you. Why would I need to lie about my job title?

🚩 #2: "You're fully licensed?" I have already confirmed that I am the new therapist which means I'm fully licensed. I have the same supervisor that you do. You and I are equal. When I assure you that I'm not an intern and I'm fully licensed, you repeat the question. I'm lying again?

🚩 #3: "You...are fully licensed." This time you're not questioning. This time I'm being challenged directly. It was masked before but now it's blatant. I am all but being asked for proof. What is wrong with me? Why can I not be fully licensed? Is it rocket science?

🚩 #4: "Oh! Well you should take over the juvenile justice kids. You should be really good with them." Now you believe me but there still has to be some way that you can condescend me. How do you know that I would be really good with the JJ kids? You don't know me and you barely believe I'm a therapist. Now, all of a sudden, I'm qualified for this particular group of kids. Why?

RED FLAG!

What is the abuse? This is very subtle mental/emotional abuse. In this particular instance this is a young black woman being challenged by an older white woman. This is covert bullying in the workplace. This type of behavior often goes unnoticed and unresolved because it seems so small. It is also easily covered up because it's the target's word against the perpetrator. If no one else heard the conversation it could be dismissed as a misunderstanding. It could be said that the perpetrator was only asking for clarity and that since the JJ kids are young and black that would make the target a good match. There would be no racial motivation assumed.

Why would a co-worker treat another co-worker this way? This type of situation happens frequently. From the start the perpetrator saw the target as beneath her simply because she was young and black. She couldn't possibly have the exact same credentials as she did. When the perpetrator finally accepted that she did have the same credentials then she found it necessary to degrade her in another way. Although it may have been true that the target might work well with the JJ kids, the perpetrator wasn't trying to be helpful. She was trying to be condescending. Since the new therapist was young and black, the same as the JJ kids, that is where she should go. She shouldn't be allowed to work in the main office doing the exact same job she's doing. That would make things too equal.

How do you recognize and avoid a situation like this? There are some who would not see this scenario in the same light that has been laid out here. That's because it's hard to prove. If no one can relate to what the new therapist is saying they may not be able to see it. Often, they refuse to see it. What you have to understand is that just because someone else doesn't see it the way you do, doesn't mean your feelings aren't valid. What you're thinking and feeling is real. Unfortunately, it's going to take quite a bit to prove it. You're going to have to figure out how to cope with the situation you have found yourself in. Can you ignore it and continue to do your job effectively? If so, do it while documenting any incidences that occur between the two of you. If it becomes too much this may be a time where you escalate up the chain of command. If you're the kind of person who likes to fight injustice, go for it. Just keep in mind that if you do this, the outcome may not be in your favor. Be prepared to find a new job if it comes to that. Do not continually subject yourself to mental/emotional abuse of any kind because it will eventually wear you down.

RED FLAG!

Subsection D: Sexual Abuse
Scenario #1

Perpetrator #1: "We're going to 'play house' and do what mommies and daddies do." 🚩 #1

Target: "I don't like this game and I don't want to play it anymore. I'm gonna tell my mom."

Perpetrator #1: "Your mom won't believe you. She needs me because I'm keeping you for free." 🚩 #2

Target: "Mom, please don't leave me alone with Uncle anymore. He's been hurting me for years and I'm sick of it!"

Perpetrator #2: "Bro! Are you touching my child?"

Perpetrator #1: "She lying! She out there being fast and blaming it on me!" 🚩 #3

Perpetrator #2: "I knew she was lying..." 🚩 #4

RED FLAG EXPLANATIONS:

🚩 #1: "We're going to 'play house' and do what

mommies and daddies do." No one should be doing what mommies and daddies do with any child! Unfortunately, it is too easy for relatives to take advantage of children. They are always around and you would assume they would not harm your children. But, the truth is...they do! Why is a grown man "playing house" with a little girl? A tea party is one thing. "House" is another!

🚩 #2: "Your mom won't believe you. She needs me because I'm keeping you for free." Here is the scare tactic that is presented to many children in this situation. She is told not to tell and that even if she does, no one will believe her. At this point she feels trapped. She is unsure of whether or not she should speak up. She is now starting to wonder if it's her fault. Shame, guilt and a lack of self-worth start to develop in this very moment. If she tells, mom loses her free babysitter. This infers that mom will be mad at her and not the uncle. In a child's mind it makes it his/her fault.

🚩 #3: "She lying! She out there being fast and blaming it on me!" Of course, when confronted, did his sister really think he would tell the truth? If this is her only source of detective work then she needs help. Did she expect that he was gonna say, "Yup! I rape your daughter every chance I get!"? Her daughter is made out to be fast and wild. But, is he not supposed to be babysitting? How is she

RED FLAG!

out there being fast on his watch? Ask some more questions mom!

🚩 **#4:** "I knew she was lying..." Yes. Mom has become Perpetrator #2 because she is now just as guilty as her brother. If mom already knew her daughter was lying, that means she had already made up in her mind that she wasn't going to believe her short of him confessing. She did not do any research. If she had paid attention to his response when she asked the question, she would have gotten the real answer. Mom asked if he had been touching her child. He never said "no". He jumped straight into accusing the child of lying and being fast. What he lead his sister to do was to assume that his answer was no. She never said her daughter told her what he did. She simply asked the question. Most people wouldn't catch that, but we need to be just that sharp when it comes things of this nature.

What is the abuse? This is sexual abuse with lasting mental/emotional effects for this girl. Since the mother didn't believe her, the sexual abuse will likely continue. Because of not being believed the child may take on the guilt, shame, a lack of self-worth and a lack of self-esteem. This can be carried into adulthood if not dealt with.

Why would an uncle and mother treat a child this

way? Perpetrator #1 is sick and believes that he can do whatever pleases him. He does not care about the well-being, thoughts, feelings or emotions of the child. He is only interested in meeting his own needs. He is comfortable with lying and manipulating situations to his benefit regardless of who it hurts. The mother does not want her life to have to change. The uncle is babysitting for free and the girl is alive each day when she comes home. It's easier for her to make the girl a liar rather than her brother. No one wants to believe their own flesh and blood could be a monster. A lying child is something that could be corrected with discipline. A child molester for a brother is unfathomable and a whole lot harder to accept and deal with.

How do you recognize and avoid a situation like this? If your child makes this type of complaint, even if you don't want to believe them, you must act as if you do. Make the report to Child Protective Services 1-800-252-5400. Also, contact the police. Let them take on the responsibility of the investigation because they are unbiased. Keep the child away from the alleged perpetrator at least until the investigation is complete. Begin counseling for the child immediately. In the event they are lying at least you will have had more than one source to make that determination. Because what if they are telling the truth and you have done nothing? Yes. All of this is an imposition to your life, but it's worth it if you can save your child from a lifetime of unnecessary pain. This is your responsibility as a parent.

RED FLAG!

Scenario #2

Perpetrator: "You're not safe at home with your mom. Come and live with us." 🚩 #1

Target: "You think Auntie would do that for me?"

Perpetrator: "Of course she will if I tell her to. You know she thinks I hung the moon." 🚩 #2

Target: "I would owe you big time if you would talk to her for me."

Perpetrator: "I'll figure out a way for you to repay me." 🚩 #3

Target: "Boys and girls don't sleep in the same bed!" 🚩 #4

Perpetrator: "We're cousins so it's fine." 🚩 #5

Target: "You raped me! Why did you do that? We're cousins!"

Perpetrator: "Remember I can do anything I want around here. You better keep your mouth shut because you don't have anywhere else to go." 🚩 #6

RED FLAG EXPLANATIONS:

🚩 **#1:** "You're not safe at home with your mom. Come and live with us." Why is she not safe at home? When home is not a safe place it often makes children unprepared to face the world. Survival mode becomes the method of operation. You learn how to stay alive instead of how to live. Pain becomes normal as your self-worth diminishes.

🚩 **#2:** "Of course she will if I tell her to. You know she thinks I hung the moon." His mom thinks he hung the moon and she will do what he tells her to do? This is a setup for him to have power over this girl if she moves into his home. She would be moving into his territory where he is king. He will override everything she does or wants to do if it's not in line with what he wants. His mother will likely take his side over hers on most occasions if it comes down to a matter of he said, she said.

🚩 **#3:** "I'll figure out a way for you to repay me." If you don't know what you will owe...don't borrow! It might boil down to a price you do not want to pay. That's all I have to say about that!

🚩 **#4:** "Boys and girls don't sleep in the same bed!" Correct! Boys and girls should not sleep in

RED FLAG!

the same bed unless that bed is a crib. In any other scenario this is just asking for trouble. In some cases, nothing might ever happen. But, why take the chance when you know the potential outcomes. If your teenaged cousin of the opposite sex is trying to sleep with you, then more than likely he/she is trying "sleep" with you! And no...there is no bias on my part that says only males are predators. A female can be a predator/perpetrator just as easily as a male.

#5: "We're cousins so it's fine." Nope! Not fine. A predator does not care if you are related to them or not. For most perpetrators a family member or family friend is easy prey. They might actually prefer to be related to you.

#6: "Remember I can do anything I want around here. You better keep your mouth shut because you don't have anywhere else to go." She feels trapped. Her own home was abusive in one way and she moved into another abusive situation with another family member. What are the chances that she will be safe with any other member of the family? If nothing is resolved or talked about in either home, he's right. She may not have any other place to go. Unfortunately, this is when we may have to consider a foster family. If your family cannot keep you safe because they are the perpetrators, then you may be better off in someone else's family. Depression and anxiety begin to set in here if they were not already present.

What is the abuse? This is sexual abuse that will likely lead to severe mental health issues. There was so much abuse in her own home that she escaped to another family member's home. Whether the abuse was worse where she came from or where she is now, only she can answer. Feeling trapped, rejected and unworthy leads to a life of survival behavior instead of learning to live.

Why would a cousin treat another cousin this way? This particular cousin gets anything he wants and treats his family like he owns them. He is getting the idea that he is more powerful than he is. He will prey upon needy people so that he always feels more powerful than they are. He will rescue her or others so that he does not have to work hard for his prey. He does not view this girl as a relative that he should value. He views her as another person in the world from which he should be able to get whatever he wants.

How do you recognize and avoid a situation like this? This family is unhealthy, but it's what she knows. This girl has to understand that not every family is like hers. She must start by telling someone what is going on. Start with a teacher or

RED FLAG!

coach. Keep in mind, they will have to report abuse to the authorities. Anyone.... child or adult who exhibits this type of behavior will not likely stop without help. If you are being harmed you must tell someone. Do not stop telling until someone believes you. You can 911 or Child Protective Services yourself at 1-800-252-5400. You may run the risk of going into the foster care system in this situation, but if no one in your family can or will protect you from harm...this may be your best option.

RED FLAG!

Scenario #3

Interviewer: "What made you decide to stay home with your dad instead of going to the store with your mom?"

Target: "He said we'd eat ice cream and play if I stayed home." 🚩 #1

Interviewer: "Is that what happened? Did you play and eat ice cream?"

Target: "At first yes. We played the tickle game and when he touched me in a place I didn't like he gave me ice cream." 🚩 #2

Interviewer: "How did your dad know he'd touched you in place you didn't like?"

Target: "Because I stopped laughing and moved away from him."

Interviewer: "Did he apologize for what happened?"

Target: "No. He said that's enough for now. We'll play again later." 🚩 #3

Interviewer: "Then what happened?"

Target: "Mom called and said she would be late and told me to take a bath before she got home."

Interviewer: "Did you do what she said?"

Target: "Yes. But, I didn't lock the door."

Interviewer: "Do you usually lock the door when you take a bath?"

Target: "No. But, my dad said that's why he came in. Because I didn't lock the door." 🚩 #4

Interviewer: "Your dad came into the bathroom while you were taking a bath?"

Target: "Yes."

Interviewer: "What happened when he came in?"

Target: "He told me that I missed a spot on my back and that he needed to wash it. That's when he hurt me." 🚩 #5

RED FLAG!

RED FLAG EXPLANATIONS:

🚩 #1: "He said we'd eat ice cream and play if I stayed home." Not all, but most parents would love a moment of peace to themselves at home. However, this dad bribed his child into staying home. You have to ask yourself why. It could be completely legit. Maybe this is a dad who works a lot and does not get to spend much time with this kid and this is just his opportunity. However, if this is not the case...

🚩 #2: "At first yes. We played the tickle game and when he touched me in a place I didn't like he gave me ice cream." This behavior can be considered "grooming". The tickle game was used to make the target comfortable with being touched. When he made his move and she caught it, he decided to stop the game and "reward" her. This gives the child the impression that nothing bad really happened. It was an accident. You're ok. We are still having a good time. Let me give you that ice cream I promised you. Many kids will forgive the incident after having a treat or at least have a different perspective of what really happened. This perspective is usually in the best interest of the perpetrator.

🚩 #3: "No. He said that's enough for now. We'll play again later." This is a warning. This is going to happen again. But, it's also a reminder to the target that we were *only* playing. This is a setup so the next time he can push it a little further.

🚩 #4: "No. But, my dad said that's why he came in. Because I didn't lock the door." Telling the child he came in because she did not lock the door is to put self-blame in her mind. It is to say that had she locked the door this would not have happened. So, maybe she asked for it. Maybe she wanted him to come in. If the target has some guilt about it and sees it as partially her fault, she is less likely to say something about it. This is a manipulative tactic.

🚩 #5: "He told me that I missed a spot on my back and that he needed to wash it. That's when he hurt me." Of course, she missed a spot on her back. It's her back! She can't see it. However, this is another tactic to subliminally put the fault on the child. If she had not missed the spot on her back then he would not have needed to touch her. He pretended to help her. In order for it not to seem out of place that he is the bathroom with his daughter, he needs to give her a reason why he's there. There may be some debate about this but there comes a certain age where fathers should not help their daughters with bath time any longer. Unfortunately, this was one of those times.

RED FLAG!

What is the abuse? This type of sexual abuse is fairly cut and dry. The perpetrator being the child's own father gave him easy access to her. The mother apparently thought nothing of leaving the daughter home with him. It's possible this is the first incident but not likely. The previous incidents just did not get this far.

Why would a father do this to his own daughter? An abuser does not care about the feelings of the person they are hurting. Some actually prefer family members. He is not looking at this girl as his flesh and blood whom he loves and should protect. He sees her as something he's entitled to. He wanted his needs met and made sure his daughter was available. Abusers of this nature can sometimes convince themselves that what they are doing is not wrong and even that the child wants it too. Some of them blame the children. She stayed home with him and she ate the ice cream. To him, that may have made it ok. Abusers are sick individuals because of their belief systems. Even when they realize they might be wrong, it does not typically make them stop.

How do you recognize and avoid a situation like this? This girl must speak out about what happened. Her mother may have missed some warning signs but now needs to know who her husband is. These incidences are often unreported and swept under a rug. Feeling strange or uneasy about it is not a reason to ignore it. Not reporting will leave her open to it happening again or even open the door to a new victim. If he got away with it once with his child, what's stop him from trying it with a niece or nephew? If you are touched inappropriately, whether it was an accident or not, report it. Say something about it no matter how insignificant you think it might be. This is not you "crying wolf". Do not put yourself in the position for it to happen again. If you do not feel comfortable or do not like playing the tickle game with your dad or whoever it might be, tell them you do not want to play. Let your mother know that you do not want to stay home with him alone. Never ignore your own thoughts, feelings, and emotions. What you think or feel is just as important as someone else's thoughts or feelings.

RED FLAG!

Subsection E: Spiritual Abuse
Scenario #1

Target: "Take me home please. I don't want to be here."

Perpetrator: "Don't you know that this was God's will?" 🚩 #1

Target: "This isn't right and I'm going to tell my aunt about this."

Perpetrator: "The Bible says all things work together for the good of those that love him. We working together in this thing." 🚩 #2

Target: "What does the Bible say about you abusing little girls?" 🚩 #3

Perpetrator: "I'm not abusing you. All throughout the books of Genesis and Exodus relatives were sleeping with each other. Hell! Amram married his daddy's sister!" 🚩 #4

Target: "You already have a wife. She's my aunt. You're only supposed to be doing this kind of stuff with her. And I'm gonna tell her."

Perpetrator: "I'm your aunt's pastor and her husband! She don't know the word like I do. Even if she did believe you she can't argue with what God told me to do with you." #5

RED FLAG EXPLANATIONS:

#1: "Don't you know that this was God's will?" What her uncle is saying is that what she wants does not matter. He and God have decided on something without her consent and she has no rights. She wanted to exercise her free will to leave. She didn't hear God speaking. All she heard was the voice of the one holding her hostage.

#2: "The Bible says all things work together for the good of those that love him. We working together in this thing." If she is not a willing participant then they are not working together. Taking scripture out of context is a plentiful habit of many clergy. If all things work together for the good of those that love Him, is he saying his target doesn't love Him? It's apparently not for her good in this moment. Or is this one of those moments where she'll understand and appreciate this later?

#3: "What does the Bible say about you abusing little girls?" Yes...quote that scripture for her please! Where in the Bible does it allow the

RED FLAG!

sexual abuse of children and say that it is pleasing to God?

🚩 **#4:** "I'm not abusing you. All throughout the books of Genesis and Exodus relatives were sleeping with each other. Hell! Amram married his daddy's sister!" Wow! A child molester who knows the Bible vs a child who is impressionable. He is both her uncle and the pastor of the church. He has convinced himself that what he is doing is ok because there was sin in the Bible. Even if he were not taking the Bible out of context, he is still breaking the law. This is still a child and even if she was willing, she is not old enough to consent.

🚩 **#5:** "I'm your aunt's pastor and her husband! She don't know the word like I do. Even if she did believe you she can't argue with what God told me to do with you." Technically this is his niece that he is molesting. He is saying that he is lord over his wife and nothing will happen if she tells. Since his wife does not know the Bible the way he does, she cannot say anything to him about what he's doing. Especially if he says God told him to do it. Beware of those who attribute things to God that He never said.

What is the abuse? This is sexual abuse backed up by spiritual abuse. In this case, the perpetrator has taken his position of authority to the extreme. He is not only her uncle but also the pastor. He is using his titles to dominate and rule over everyone in the family and possibly the church.

Why would an uncle treat his niece this way? This is not uncommon. This type of behavior runs through families and generations of families. He is doing it because he can. No one can tell him anything because he's the pastor. Being his niece means absolutely nothing. The target is easy access to him. He is a child molester who also has access to the parishioners of his church as well. He is looked up to for leadership and people follow him simply because he is supposed to be God's representative. Who wants to believe that the "pastor" would do this to his own niece?

How do you recognize and avoid a situation like this? This behavior is wrong on every level. The target realizes that it's wrong, but she may be stuck in the situation. If she thinks her aunt will not believe her then who does she turn to? Are her parents living? If they are, that is the first place she needs to run to. If not, she needs to be strategic about who she tells because of who he is. There are many that would label her a troublemaker rather than help her. It will backfire on her quickly if she does not get to the right person. Her school system must contact the authorities if she tells in that environment, so that would be a good avenue. However, in this situation, going into the system is likely if there is no other relative safe enough to take guardianship. She needs a safety plan immediately.

RED FLAG!

Scenario #2

Target: "Hello?"

Perpetrator: "I knew you wasn't no good! God told me!" 🚩 #1

Target: "Look Valerie...I'm really trying to be nice so please stop calling my phone."

Perpetrator: "It's Minister Valerie to you!"

Target: "You want to be recognized by a title you don't operate in?"

Perpetrator: "If you hang up in my face again God gone send you straight to hell because He don't like you no way!" 🚩 #2

Target: "Well, I guess I'll meet you there because you been doing the same thing I've been doing."

Perpetrator: "You ain't got nothing to say about what I'm doing because the Bible says, "touch not my anointed and do my prophet no harm!" 🚩 #3

Target: "You ain't better than nobody else! How are we doing the same exact thing but you saved and I'm not?"

Perpetrator: "Because I'm anointed! The Bible says all my sins are forgiven so it don't matter what I do cause God already forgave me!" 🚩 #4

Target: "So, He can forgive you but not me?" 🚩 #5

Perpetrator: "Yes! Because you got a unclean spirit!" 🚩 #6

RED FLAG EXPLANATIONS:

🚩 #1: "I knew you wasn't no good! God told me!" Be careful here. God does not condemn... He convicts. It is possible that God could have given her warning to steer clear of a person. However, the way it is being presented here is meant to condemn, judge and attack.

🚩 #2: "If you hang up in my face again God gone send you straight to hell because He don't like you no way!" Whoa! Does God not give chances? Is that not why He sent Jesus? Would He really send someone straight to hell because He doesn't like them? He sure does seem to tell this "minister" a lot of awful things about this target. She is putting her thoughts and feelings on the situation and attributing them to God. She is making God sound like a scary, hateful God rather than a loving one.

🚩 **#3:** "You ain't got nothing to say about what I'm doing because the Bible says, "touch not my anointed and do my prophet no harm!" Yes, the Bible does say that. Yet, this "minister" never stopped to ask whether she was violating that very ordinance herself? How does she know that her target is not anointed or a prophet? Our dislike of someone has no bearing on the way God feels about them. The perpetrator is taking a portion of the Bible and making herself untouchable because she has deemed her target unworthy. But, has God actually deemed her target unworthy?

🚩 **#4:** "Because I'm anointed! The Bible says all my sins are forgiven so it don't matter what I do cause God already forgave me!" It does matter what you do. This type of behavior is not showing love, which God has commanded us to do. Sure, He will forgive us if we confess our sins, repent and turn from them. This perpetrator is using the forgiveness of sins as cart blanc to do whatever she wants. She deems anything she does as OK because she is "anointed" and is already forgiven. Forgiveness is not a free ticket to hurt people.

🚩 **#5:** "So, He can forgive you but not me?" Good question! If God is no respecter of persons then everybody can be forgiven.

🚩 **#6:** "Yes! Because you got a unclean spirit!" Wow! The perpetrator has just told the target that she cannot be forgiven because she has an unclean spirit. She has condemned this girl to hell, told her God does not like her and all of this while claiming to be a minister of the gospel. Is it not part of her work to help rid her of the unclean spirit or get her to someone who can?

What is the abuse? This is spiritual abuse. This minister has taken her title to mean that she is above her target. She is actually exuding the opposite of what she should be. She is showing hatred instead of love and doing it in the name of God.

Why would a minister treat anyone this way? It is easy for some to see the faults in others but not in themselves. This perpetrator uses her title of minister as a pass for her behavior. She feels that because she will be forgiven she can treat people she does not like any way she wants and get away with it. She twists the word to benefit only her in this situation because she expects that the target does not know it for herself.

RED FLAG!

How do you recognize and avoid a situation like this? Know the Word for yourself. If you know what the Bible says, then you will know when someone is using it out of context. Have a relationship with God so that you know for yourself when you are out of alignment. Understand that God does not want to condemn you to hell. He wants to convict you to repentance so that you will get back into alignment. Be extremely cautious of anyone who would wish ill upon you and say that it is coming from God. You do not have to challenge them. You only need to know what God says about you. If this is a minister in your church, the pastor needs to know what is going on. If this person *is* your pastor, this is probably not the right church for you.

RED FLAG!

Scenario #3

Perpetrator: "I am building a new foundation and a new church."

Target: "Oh wow! What is your vision for the new church?"

Perpetrator: "That is not your place to question. You just need to follow." 🚩 #1

Target: "For now I just want to observe. I'm not sure I trust you yet."

Perpetrator: "I am God's favorite. If you're not with me God will deal with you." 🚩 #2

Target: "Oh!"

Perpetrator: "I only need people here who are on board and will answer yes and amen to whatever I ask." 🚩 #3

Target: "I can't just follow you blindly when I don't have a clue of what you're doing."

Perpetrator: "I don't have time to teach you. You have to read the word for yourself." 🚩 #4

Target: "I do read the word and it doesn't tell me

to follow you off a cliff."

Perpetrator: "If you don't follow my lead that will put you outside God's will and you will not be blessed!" 🚩 #5

RED FLAG EXPLANATIONS:

🚩 **#1:** "That is not your place to question. You just need to follow." Even God allows us to question. You might not like the answer you get, but you can ask. Most people who do not want to answer questions either do not know the answers or are so arrogant that you offend them by asking. Be leery of anyone who simply wants you to follow blindly without any understanding.

🚩 **#2:** "I am God's favorite. If you're not with me God will deal with you." What? God's favorite? I get being favored. But, saying that you are God's favorite insinuates that I am beneath you or at the most I am second best. That is just like saying that your mother has a favorite child. Unfortunately, there are some mothers who do that. But, God does not. We can all be favored. Calling yourself His favorite also tells me that you are a jealous person. What would you do to me if God blessed

RED FLAG!

me with something you wanted? If He showed favor toward me regarding that thing before you got it, how would you treat me?

🚩 **#3:** "I only need people here who are on board and will answer yes and amen to whatever I ask." Answering yes and Amen to everything someone asks is dangerous. Being a people-pleaser does not work because you can never please everyone. If you answer yes and Amen to everything someone wants you will find yourself in trouble. You will begin to deny yourself and go against your own will and maybe even God's. If you told your child "yes" every time they asked for something, what kind of person do you think they would turn out to be? It's the same thing here. There would be absolutely no balance in the life of a person if everyone around them always said yes.

🚩 **#4:** "I don't have time to teach you. You have to read the word for yourself." You don't have time to teach me? But, you're the pastor. Is that not what you do? Not just for me, but the entire congregation. Of course, I should read the word for myself so I know what you're teaching me. However, if you do not have time to teach me then why am I coming to your church? I could stay at home and watch someone else on TV. If I'm a member of your congregation I should be able to trust you so that I can follow you.

🚩 #5: "If you don't follow my lead that will put you outside God's will and you will not be blessed!" Now you're condemning me for not following you. I cannot follow you because I do not understand and I do not trust you. You have no time for me and now I will not be blessed? You are beginning to sound more and more like a cult leader every time you open your mouth. You only want me around if I answer yes to everything you ask. I am to follow you without question even though I do not know where you're going. You are God's favorite so that makes me what? I can only be blessed if I do what you say?

What is the abuse? This is spiritual abuse. The pastor wants something that even God does not demand. She wants people to follow her lead blindly and not have free will. She wants her will to be done. She is out for herself regardless of what happens to the people in the church. If they follow her they will be blessed. If not, woe be unto them!

Why would a pastor treat a church member this way? Power and arrogance are a dangerous combination. When a person is out for the benefit of themselves it does not matter what anyone else thinks or feels. The power that goes along with the title is maddening for some. There are some who should not be in power because they cannot handle it. They will throw anyone under a bus without hesitation if necessary. Pastor is just a word if you do not honor the responsibility attached to it.

How do you recognize and avoid a situation like this? Gut check. If you are under the leadership of someone you do not trust, that is a problem. Your pastor should be someone you can talk to without feeling condemned. You may certainly feel convicted to make a change and do better. But, you should not feel helpless and trapped. Your decision should always be your own. If someone has taken your right to make a decision, that's a problem as well. If you are in a situation where you have no trust, no understanding and no rights, get out of it.

RED FLAG!

Subsection F: Self-Harm
Scenario #1

Friend: "I haven't seen you in a couple of weeks. How are you feeling?"

Target: "Oh! I'm great. I just came by to drop off something to you."

Friend: "Well...the last time I saw you, you were super depressed. Are you better?" #1

Target: "Yes! I'm all better. As a matter of fact, I'm doing so well that I'm going on a trip!" #2

Friend: "Really? Where you going?"

Target: "I'm just gonna get away for a couple of days. Nowhere in particular." #3

Friend: "Ok. Well...what were you coming to drop off to me?"

Target: "Look! I brought you this black dress that you love so much!"

Friend: "But that's your favorite dress and you're supposed to wear it to the dance next month."
 #4

Target: "Yeah I know. But, I want you to have it. I know you love it!"

Friend: "Well...thanks! Who are you going on your trip with again?"

Target: "I'm going by myself..." #5

RED FLAG EXPLANATIONS:

#1: "Well...the last time I saw you, you were super depressed. Are you better?" If someone you know is "super depressed", do not go weeks without hearing from them. People who are dealing with severe depression should not be alone. They should be seeking treatment.

#2: "Yes! I'm all better. As a matter of fact, I'm doing so well that I'm going on a trip!" Huge RED FLAG! If she was very depressed the last time you saw her and now she is "all better", this should alarm you. Depression does not usually dissipate all at once. Certainly, if it has been a while since you saw them you could have simply missed the progression. However, getting better all of a sudden is a Red Flag! because it often indicates that the person has come up with a plan to take the pain away. This is what makes them feel better.

🚩 **#3:** "I'm just gonna get away for a couple of days. Nowhere in particular." Going on a trip with no real plans? Be suspicious of this. It may signify not wanting to be contacted or found. It is surely not uncommon for people to just need to get away from their day-to-day life on occasion. But, with someone who has recently been very depressed it's just not a good idea.

🚩 **#4:** "But that's your favorite dress and you're supposed to wear it to the dance next month." Giving away prized possessions or favorite items may seem very kind. In this case however, it is a tell-tell sign of a memorial. You are receiving a gift to remember them by and of course because they no longer have a need for it.

🚩 **#5:** "I'm going by myself..." If you have not caught any of the flags up to now, this is the one you cannot afford to miss. Going on a trip to nowhere in particular...alone. Not good! I hope you know by now that this is an attempted suicide in the making. You have no idea of how to reach them if they do not answer the phone and there will be no one around to witness what happens.

What is the abuse? If there is no intervention, this may either be an attempted or committed suicide. For the purposes of this book, it is considered an abuse against yourself. To take your life is an act of violence committed against your own body.

Why would a person treat themselves this way? Typically, there are mental health and/or self-esteem issues at work. Depression, overwhelming sadness and pain play huge roles. Feeling hopeless, trapped and helpless with no sign of relief can bring anyone to the end of their rope. Suicide is sometimes seen as the only answer. They may feel like they have tried everything else. Ending their lives would mean the end to the pain they are experiencing.

How do you recognize and avoid a situation like this? Do not take anything for granted. If you see a loved one who just cannot seem to get it together do not assume it will pass. If they complain of unbearable pain, whether physically or emotionally, pay attention. Encourage them to seek help. Offer to go with them. Do not expect or make them solely responsible for doing it on their own. Sometimes it's the isolation and feeling so alone that is feeding the desire not to live. Check out the National Suicide Prevention Lifeline at www.suicidepreventionlifeline.org or call 800-273-8255.

RED FLAG!

Scenario #2

Target's Mom: "I can't get my daughter to wear dresses and sandals for nothing!"

Friend: "What does she like to wear?"

Target's Mom: "All she ever wears are hoodies and crew socks...even in summer!" 🚩 #1

Friend: "Well...what does she like to wear around the house?"

Target's Mom: "Hoodies and crew socks!" 🚩 #2

Friend: "Is that what all her friends are wearing? Do you feel like it's normal teenage stuff?"

Target's Mom: "I guess so but I have not seen that girl show any skin in a year. She used to love to wear cute little nighties. Now she even comes out of the shower fully dressed!" 🚩 #3

Friend: "It's probably just a phase. She'll grow out of it." 🚩 #4

Target's Mom: "I sure hope so. I'll be glad when she stops moping around and turns back into my happy little girl again." 🚩 #5

RED FLAG EXPLANATIONS:

🚩 **#1:** "All she ever wears are hoodies and crew socks…even in summer!" If your child is wearing hoodies and crew socks even in summer there may be an issue. It could just be what she likes, but do take notice. This is a sign of a cover up, literally. At the least, it could be a sign of depression.

🚩 **#2:** "Hoodies and crew socks!" Most people do not lounge around the house fully dressed. If your child has on hoodies and crew socks even at home this should raise suspicion. It is possible that she is having body image issues or maybe something deeper.

🚩 **#3:** "I guess so but I have not seen that girl show any skin in a year. She used to love to wear cute little nighties. Now she even comes out of the shower fully dressed!" This could very well be slightly normal for teenagers. The truth is, sometimes teens are a little peculiar. However, there is nothing normal about coming out of the shower fully dressed. Especially, if she used to love cute sleepwear. A change in style is to be expected. A change in personality is suspect.

🚩 **#4:** "It's probably just a phase. She'll grow out of it." The friend may be right. It could be a phase. The problem with it is that with so many young people going into phases and never coming out, this behavior is still a cause for alarm.

#5: "I sure hope so. I'll be glad when she stops moping around and turns back into my happy little girl again." Bingo! She's moping around and not being her usual self. She used to be a happy little girl who has changed into a different person. Depression and anxiety look different in children and teens than they do in adults.

What is the abuse? At this point it is just based on signs, symptoms and suspicion. But, if my suspicion is correct, this girl is cutting herself. The abuse is considered self-harm or self-injury. It is possible that she has stopped showing skin because she is hiding the scars. At the very least, this is a child who is experiencing depression or some type of internal turmoil.

Why would a person treat themselves this way? Cutting, as well as other types of self-harming behaviors are most often a sign of mental health issues in a young person. This may sound strange, but to a person who is in deep emotional pain, physical pain helps them feel better. It allows them to be in control. Even though it is a hidden behavior, it is a cry for help. This is someone who is in pain and has not been able to figure out another way to fix it. If untreated, the next phase could be a suicide attempt.

How do you recognize and avoid a situation like this? This behavior is difficult for most parents to understand because it is a physical behavior that is rooted in an emotional battle. Just like in this scenario, if you notice your child only wearing long sleeves no matter what season, that is your first indication of possible self-injuring behavior. However, in order to catch it before that, you will look for signs of emotional changes. Watch for changes in attitude, friends, eating and sleeping habits, music and style of dress. These things may seem insignificant and normal for a teenager, but you need to ask questions. Do not just assume that this is a normal phase. If you catch them cutting their arms and they start wearing short sleeves...start checking other body parts. Just because they stop injuring themselves in one area does not mean they have stopped the behavior. It could just mean they relocated to throw you off. Legs and feet are alternative places to cut. If you do find evidence of self-harming behavior, this is a child who needs help. Do not try to handle this alone. If this is a family related issue, do not shy away from the entire family needing to be in treatment.

RED FLAG!

Scenario #3

Target: "I think I have a problem with weed…"

Counselor: "Do you think you have a problem or did someone tell you that you do?"

Target: "Both." 🚩 #1

Counselor: "Ok. Can you tell me about how much you smoke?"

Target: "All day, every day." 🚩 #2

Counselor: "Does it affect you on your job?"

Target: "By the end of the day I get pretty anxious, so I know I need to get straight home and smoke. Other than that, it really only affects me more in my personal life." 🚩 #3

Counselor: "How so?"

Target: "Well…I have all these great ideas about things I want to do. But, when I start smoking it all goes out the window."

Counselor: "How does it all go out the window?"

Target: "Because I don't care about anything anymore. As long as I have my weed I don't need anything else." 🚩 #4

Counselor: "Do you want to quit smoking?"

Target: "I can't!" 🚩 #5

Counselor: "What makes you feel like you can't quit?"

Target: "I tried before and I almost went crazy!" 🚩 #6

RED FLAG EXPLANATIONS:

🚩 **#1:** "Both." If you think you have a problem and another loved one has mentioned it as well…likely there is a problem. If you are willing to admit it then you may be ready to make the necessary changes.

🚩 **#2:** "All day, every day." If you are smoking weed all day, every day there is definitely an issue. This is where you move from recreation to addiction.

RED FLAG!

#3: "By the end of the day I get pretty anxious, so I know I need to get straight home and smoke. Other than that, it really only it affects me more in my personal life." If you are getting anxious by the end of the day this could mean one of two things and maybe both. Not being able to smoke for several hours with an addiction may cause withdrawal symptoms. Also, there may be an underlying mental health issue such as anxiety. It could be that you suffer from anxiety and began using the weed to self-medicate.

#4: "Because I don't care about anything anymore. As long as I have my weed I don't need anything else." Being laid back and not caring about anything is not an uncommon side effect of smoking. The problem comes into place where you get stuck in your life and cannot make progress because of the smoking.

#5: "I can't!" This signifies the addiction. If you want to but cannot do it on your own, then you need help. It's ok to ask for help. You will not be arrested for seeking treatment. Just do not show up to any facility with the product on your person.

#6: "I tried before and I almost went crazy!" If you have tried before, it likely means you realized a while ago that you had a problem that you wanted to get rid of. Not having the support you needed is likely the reason why you were unsuccessful. Again, you do not have to do this on your own. You almost went crazy because you likely tried to quit cold turkey. If you have an underlying mental health issue that you were covering up with the weed, you still need treatment for the mental health issue as well.

What is the abuse? Self-medicating, which has lead to substance dependence, is considered the abuse in this scenario. This is because you are using a substance to help you cope with an underlying issue rather than dealing with the real issue. This is the same as being an alcoholic. Using a substance to cover up issues will just cause more issues.

Why would a person treat themselves this way? It is still difficult for some to admit they have mental health issues. In the case of smoking weed, it could be looked at as something everybody does. So, what's the big deal? The big deal is that not everybody who smokes has an addiction to it. Maybe this person does not know the difference.

How do you recognize and avoid a situation like this? Pay attention to what happens to you when you smoke and what happens when you do not. Is it something you do for fun, could you take it or

RED FLAG!

leave it, or is it something you need? If you fall in the category where you feel you need it, ask yourself more questions. Why do you need it? What is it doing for you? Is there anything else that you can think of that would give you what you need if you were to take away the weed? The answers to these questions will tell you a great deal. Be honest about the other issues you have. Smoking can help mask the other issues because you can get high enough not to have to think about them. The only problem with this is that the other issues never get resolved. Ignoring them does not make them go away. It simply covers them up for a while. Ultimately, you need to smoke more and more weed to keep covering it up. Or, you move onto other things to help. You can do that by using more negative coping mechanisms, which will probably lead to trouble. Or, you get help and learn positive coping mechanisms so that you regain control of your life.

RED FLAG!

PART II
BEING PLAYED BY YOUR MIND

RED FLAG!

Triggers Section #1: Past Events/Trauma

The working definition of a "Trigger" in this book is something that causes a painful memory to come from the past into the present.

What is Trauma? Merriam-Webster gives several fitting definitions for trauma.

a: an injury (such as a wound) to living tissue caused by an extrinsic agent
b: a disordered psychic or behavioral state resulting from severe mental or emotional stress or physical injury
c: an emotional upset

Who experiences trauma? Anyone who has been through an unexpected event that caused severe distress. This includes but is not limited to a car accident, death of a loved one, rape, etc.

Why are traumas triggered? Often, traumatic incidents go without being treated due to the painful nature. No one wants to relive a trauma, so we hesitate to talk about it. Unresolved traumatic memories are stored and sometimes locked in the brain. The triggers are like keys that unlock the memories.

Characteristics of Unresolved Trauma: There are many signs of unresolved trauma, but here are a few. Feeling worthless and of no value or importance, chronic and repeated suicidal thoughts and feelings, failed attempts at suicide, frequent intensely dysfunctional relationships, inappropriate responsibility and self-blame, anxiety, depression, flashbacks and/or nightmares are all common.

How does one resolve trauma? Resolving trauma begins with acknowledgment that there was a traumatic event in your life that is still affecting you. For many, there are several traumatic events that can sometimes be difficult to differentiate. Prayer, counseling, medication and support groups can be highly effective. Trauma resolution is intense work because there are usually a number of unknown triggers that cause reactions. Do not attempt to do this work alone.

This next section gives real life examples of traumatic events being triggered. It includes highlights of potential Red Flags as well as Trigger indications that are often missed in situations such as these. Because there can be many triggers to just one incident they can be difficult to pinpoint. Triggers often seem to "come out nowhere". They may appear to have nothing to do with what is going on with you in the very moment, but with

RED FLAG!

work and understanding they can be figured out. Pay close attention to what sets people off because you may need to be able to de-escalate or diffuse a situation at any moment.

RED FLAG!

Scenario #1

Client Background: This is a 36-year old female with a past history of physical, mental, sexual and spiritual abuse. The abuse began in her childhood home. She grew up with an abusive, alcoholic father. He was physically and mentally abusive toward her mother and all of the children. Once she left home, she was raped and emotionally, mentally and physically abused in each relationship she entered. She became an alcoholic herself in order to escape all the pain she had to endure. She began to give her body away so that she would be in control of it, rather than to have someone take it from her again. After beginning counseling, she stopped drinking and became celibate as a part of her healing process.

Counselor: "You look a bit distressed. How was your week?"

Client: "I went to visit my boyfriend and his mother last week. It started out fine but quickly went wrong."

Counselor: "What happened?"

Client: "He got mad at his mom right before we were supposed to go out to dinner. He storms out of the house and takes off down the road with me and my best friend in the car. He scared both of us to death with the way he was driving!" 🚩 #1

Counselor: "Were you able to talk to him about what was going on with him?"

Client: "No! As soon as we got to the restaurant he started throwing back drinks! My friend said something once he got to the third one because she was concerned." 🚩 #2 🚪🚪🚪 #1

Counselor: "How were you feeling watching him do this and hearing what your friend had to say?"

Client: "I was pissed! I told him that I would be driving us back home. Then he has the nerve to say that since I was driving back home he could turn up!" 🚩 #3

Counselor: "He didn't consider three drinks turning up?"

Client: "No! He proceeds to tell me that he used to drink a lot more than this and that he could handle it. When we got back to the house his mom confirmed it. All I knew was that I was ready to go home." 🚩 #4

Counselor: "Well, how did the night finally end? Did you ever have an opportunity to talk to him

RED FLAG!

about how it made you feel to see him act like that?"

Client: "The night ended with us getting into an argument about his behavior. His mom jumps in to try to calm me down and says "this is just your first fight". When I said I wanted to go home he calmed down. Of course, then he thought it would be a good idea to try to get me to have sex with him after I told him I wasn't having sex." #5 #2

Counselor: "Do you think this is a person you should be in a relationship with? I'm hearing several red flags that are concerning."

Client: "Well, he made me mad but I love him. I hope we can work things out." #6

RED FLAG EXPLANATIONS:

#1: "He got mad at his mom right before we were supposed to go out to dinner. He storms out of the house and takes off down the road with me and my best friend in the car. He scared both of us to death with the way he was driving!" He got mad at his mom and storms out of the house instead of working things out with her. Then he drives recklessly with his girlfriend and her friend in the car. So, not only does he endanger their lives but his and others on the road with him. All because he's mad? He is showing her his temper and what his potential future behavior might be like when his temper rears its ugly head.

#2: "No! As soon as we got to the restaurant he started throwing back drinks! My friend said something once he got to the third one because she was concerned." Her boyfriend uses alcohol to deal with his emotions. That is a negative coping mechanism. She has to ask herself if this is what will happen in their relationship whenever he is mad with her. Is this someone she will have to worry and wonder about what he is doing and whether or not he is ok every time he leaves the house? Even if she is not concerned, her friend sure is.

#3: "I was pissed! I told him that I would be driving us back home. Then he has the nerve to say that since I was driving back home he could turn up!" Now he can turn up? He basically just told her that throwing back several drinks within a matter of minutes is nothing. Having had a problem with alcohol abuse herself, being with someone who drinks is a problem. In this situation she can only hope that he is a happy drunk and not an aggressive one like her father was. She can only hope he knows when to stop. But, what if he doesn't?

#4: "No! He proceeds to tell me that he used to drink a lot more than this and that he could handle it. When we got back to the house his mom confirmed it. All I knew was that I was ready to go home." Confirmed! He used to drink a lot more. While it is great that he has possibly slowed down, he is still drinking a lot more than his girlfriend is comfortable with. He likely only stopped when he did because she and her friend voiced their concerns. Does she really want to take the chance of risking her safety in order to find out if he knows when to stop on his own?

#5: "The night ended with us getting into an argument about his behavior. His mom jumps in to try to calm me down and says "this is just your first fight". When I said I wanted to go home he calmed down. Of course, then he thought it would be a good idea to try to get me to have sex with him after I told him I wasn't having sex." His mom jumps into their fight? This is JUST your FIRST fight? Not only does she now have a meddling mother-in-law, but she has just told her that there will be many more fights to come. Who would know first-hand better than his mother, whom he just got into a fight with earlier in the evening that set this whole night in motion? He calms down only when she threatens to leave. Then, as if nothing has happened, he attempts to get her to have sex when she made it clear that she was not ready.

#6: "Well, he made me mad but I love him. I hope we can work things out." She has fallen in love with her past. He is a drinker who needs to have sex. Currently, she is neither of those things but she used to be. How does she expect to maintain the progress she has made in her healing process when she is in a relationship with a replica of her past? He may have great qualities and she may love him but she is playing with fire. If she wants to marry her father, he is staring her in the face. She just doesn't see it.

RED FLAG!

TRIGGER EXPLANATIONS:

#1: "No! As soon as we got to the restaurant he started throwing back drinks! My friend said something once he got to the third one because she was concerned." She is sober after years of drinking to numb her own pain. Now, she is in a relationship with someone who uses alcohol to handle his emotions. How long does she think she'll be able to remain sober with someone who drinks irresponsibly?

#2: "The night ended with us getting into an argument about his behavior. His mom jumps in to try to calm me down and says "this is just your first fight". When I said I wanted to go home he calmed down. Of course, then he thought it would be a good idea to try to get me to have sex with him after I told him I wasn't having sex." She grew up watching her parents fight. Almost every relationship she got into before now she had to fight for her own life. Currently, she is being presented with a boyfriend who she has spent two days with and they are already fighting.

This may not be a Red Flag! to her because she's used to the behavior, but it is a trigger that could send her back into her previous behavior. On top of this, she is celibate but he is not. She spent her life fighting people off of her that would not take "no" for an answer. She started giving up her body so they would stop taking it from her. Not that he would rape her but how long does she think she can remain celibate when she is dating someone who is not? Either she is going to give in or he is going to cheat. He might be waiting for her but he is not waiting with her.

RED FLAG!

Scenario #2

Perpetrator Background: This is a 25 - year old male with a past history of verbal and mental abuse. His father called him stupid so much that he almost thought it was his name. He actually answered to it whenever his father yelled, "Hey Stupid!" He was teased as a child and bullied throughout most of his life. Even though he got straight A's in school, he felt stupid. He always felt inferior to other guys until he got into college. Girls liked him because he was smart. However, he always got put in the "friend zone" because of his lack of social skills. When he finally got a girlfriend, he vowed it would be forever.

Target: Received a compliment from the waiter on how beautiful she was. #1

Perpetrator: Became irate because he felt like he had been disrespected. #1

Target: Reassured her boyfriend that she only had eyes for him but that she couldn't stop someone from complimenting her.

Perpetrator: Grabbed her by her arm, pulled her out of the restaurant and pushed her into the car. #2

Target: Insisted that if they were going to be together he was going to have to trust her. #3

Perpetrator: "Shut up or I'll wrap this car around a tree and kill us both!" #4

Target: "Don't be stupid…" #2

Perpetrator: "I'm not stupid!" He grabbed her head and slammed it into the window. #5

Target: Woke up in the hospital unable to move.

Perpetrator: Wrapped the car around a tree and killed himself and severely wounded his date.

RED FLAG EXPLANATIONS:

#1: Became irate because he felt like he had been disrespected: True…this may have been a disrespectful move by the waiter. However, becoming irate is a bigger problem. Simply addressing the disrespect would have been appropriate. His excessive anger may indicate that he is dealing with pride, control and ownership issues stemming from his damaged self-esteem.

RED FLAG!

His feelings were hurt that his date accepted a compliment from another man and appeared to like it. To a man who struggles with self-esteem, this quickly brings his mind to insecurity. He may feel that any man who compliments his woman could potentially steal her from him. He becomes irate because he does not cope with his emotions well and it scares people. It can also be used as a show of force. He appears strong in his anger.

#2: Grabbed her by her arm, pulled her out of the restaurant and pushed her into the car: He is escalating. She was not scared by his anger so he moves into what he believes to be a stronger show of force. She is likely smaller than he is so she can be physically manipulated. If this is how he reacts in public, she should be concerned about being alone with him. Because he is unable to de-escalate, she needs to.

#3: Insisted that if they were going to be together he was going to have to trust her: Once you realize he has trust issues that lead to public outbursts, understand that this is not someone you want to try and have a relationship with at this time. He is not ready and nothing you do will get him there. He has to recognize and want it for himself. You are setting yourself up for a nightmare.

#4: "Shut up or I'll wrap this car around a tree and kill us both!" You hope he is not serious because he did not appear suicidal when you started the date, but you must take this seriously. He is continuing to escalate and you need to believe what he is saying to you. He is angry, he is hurting and he is becoming irrational.

#5: "I'm not stupid!" He grabbed her head and slammed it into the window: He has reached his limit with the situation. He has gone from trying to regain control to abuse. He is now completely out of control and the only way to regain it is to follow through with his threat. He is not getting the reaction he wants and needs from you. He is unable to de-escalate and at this point he may not want to. In his mind you deserve punishment and he does not care if he is a casualty in the process.

TRIGGER EXPLANATIONS:

#1: Received a compliment from the waiter on how beautiful she was: The waiter became a threat immediately. This is the first girl that he has gotten to be with him and actually go out with him. Everyone else put him in the "friend

RED FLAG!

zone" and dated other guys. He still feels inferior because of his lack of social skills. If she is paying attention to someone else then he could lose her too. He is sick of being in the "friend zone".

#2: "Don't be stupid..." His father called him stupid all his life. Then, the one girl he finally gets to go out with him seriously calls him stupid too! That's not actually what she meant but that is what he heard. She humiliated him in the restaurant and called him stupid on top of that.

RED FLAG!

Scenario #3

Client Background: This is a 42 - year old female who grew up in a verbally and emotionally abusive family. She was the oldest of 6 children. Her father left when she was young because he could do nothing right in her mother's eyes. The words that spewed from her mother's lips were venomous. This client became the golden child because she was the oldest, the smartest and the most self-sufficient. But, that title and prestige came with a price. It meant she had to be perfect or she would be lumped back in with everyone else. The love/hate relationship her mother developed with her was born out of jealousy and pride. Pride that her daughter was doing so well but jealous in that she could not have it for herself.

Client: "I'm calling off my engagement!"

Counselor: "What's going on? What would make you call off the engagement?"

Client: "He's gonna make me lose everything I've worked so hard for!" #1, #1

Counselor: "What do you mean? What has he done wrong?"

Client: "He charged up some stuff on a credit card

and he owes back child support!"

Counselor: "Ok. He's not as good with money as you. Is that not something you can help him with?"

Client: "Yes but...he drinks too!"  #3

Counselor: "What scares you about the things he does?"

Client: "He's so nonchalant. It's like he doesn't care." #3

Counselor: "What do you really believe about him? Do you believe he cares?"

Client: "I think he does but I need him to be more like me." #4

Counselor: "You have a fear of failure and he doesn't. Do you want him to live in fear like you?"

Client: "Of course not. I wish I could be more like him in that way. I want to trust him with my life, but I can't." #4

Counselor: "Why can't you?"

Client: "Because I don't know how to trust. #5

RED FLAG!

Counselor: "So, would you rather live without him or learn how to trust him?"

RED FLAG EXPLANATIONS:

#1: "He's gonna make me lose everything I've worked so hard for!" If it is a true statement that he is going to make her lose everything then she is correct in re-evaluating the relationship. However, fear-based decisions are often not well-thought out decisions. Making sure you are looking at something clearly is important. Acting out of fear can cloud your judgment. She has a fear of failure that is playing a major role here.

#2: "He charged up some stuff on a credit card and he owes back child support!" Is there is no room for error? Does he realize that he made a mistake in charging the cards? Was there an emergency situation where he needed to do that? Many people get behind on their child support. Are these real reasons for breaking up or is there a different underlying issue?

#3: "Yes but...he drinks too!" Does she feel he drinks too much or is it just the fact that he drinks at all? She must ask herself whether or not these are issues of being controlling on her part or does he really have major issues? The things he does appear to be too much for her to handle. He has too many issues that may do damage to the health of their relationship. It could also unmask the façade of being perfect that she feels the need to keep up.

#4: "I think he does but I need him to be more like me." She must realize that she will not be able to change his personality. She started dating a man who was nothing like her. It's probably what she liked about him. Now, she needs him to change so that she can be at peace. If he were truly more like her, they would both be high strung and stressed.

#5: "Because I don't know how to trust." If she does not trust the man she is supposed to marry, what kind of relationship do they really have? She doesn't know how to trust because she never learned. Learning to trust is difficult. You have to know what characteristics you need to see in a person in order to know if they are trustworthy in your eyes. The only thing she ever saw was her mother being in control. If you are always in control, you have no need to trust anyone.

RED FLAG!

TRIGGER EXPLANATIONS:

#1: "He's gonna make me lose everything I've worked so hard for!" She is going into protective mode. This is not necessarily a bad thing, but she is used to having to do things on her own. She needs to be perfect and if he is going to cause her to lose her perfect record, he has to go. Feelings are not important in this situation. It does not matter whether they love each other or not. If there is a possibility that he may do something to change the way other people view her, he gets sacrificed. This could be the reason her parents divorced.

#2: "He charged up some stuff on a credit card and he owes back child support!" Her father could never do anything right in the eyes of her mother. She does not realize that she is now carrying that behavior and mindset into her relationship. If he's behind in child support make a plan to help him get back on track. She must learn to accept the fact that people make mistakes.

#3: "He's so nonchalant. It's like he doesn't care." Her father was likely a laid-back man because her mother was so uptight. She does not realize that she is probably attracted to him for the same reasons her mother was originally attracted to her father. She loves her father and she has chosen a man who is similar to him. However, her mother dominated him and drove him away. She's doing the same whether she realizes it or not.

#4: "Of course not. I wish I could be more like him in that way. I want to trust him with my life, but I can't." Trusting someone else with your life would mean you would have to give up some control. You cannot give up control if you have a fear of failure. You will never have faith in anyone but yourself to ensure things are perfect. Because he is more laid-back, he does not have the same intensity she does about things so she will never trust him completely. And the truth is, if he were more high-strung like she is, they would likely become aggressive toward each other.

RED FLAG!

Triggers Section #2: Senses

What is a sense? Merriam-Webster gives this definition.

a. the facility of perceiving by means of sense organs
b: a specialized function or mechanism (such as sight, hearing, smell, taste, or touch) by which an animal receives and responds to external or internal stimuli
c: the sensory mechanisms constituting a unit distinct from other functions (such as movement or thought)

Who has senses? Not everyone has all five senses working effectively, but everyone has at least some of them. There are those who have lost one or more of their senses due to health issues or birth deformities. However, typically when one sense is lost or diminished, the other senses become stronger. For example, if you have ever seen the movie *Ray* about the life of Ray Charles, you noticed that as he lost his sight his senses of hearing and touch magnified.

Why are senses important when discussing triggers? Information from the outside world is received through our senses and then carried to the brain. When an offense is committed against you, the trauma comes in through your senses and the incident is stored in your brain. For example, if you have been physically abused the most obvious sense is touch, even though there may be other senses involved as well. Your skin will send a pain signal to your brain and store it. Going forward, even the slightest touch to that same area might bring back the memory of being hit or grabbed.

How does one use senses to understand and/or resolve triggers? If you do not remember the trauma or believe you have resolved it, your senses will put your mind to the test. They can be used to help you recall a trauma or they can notify you that there is an unresolved trauma still lurking. Once you identify a trigger through your senses, you must process through the past incident until you are "safe" from it. This may mean placing boundaries around people, places and things. It may also mean implementing different practices for your life in every effort to bring resolve to the situation, both past and present.

This next session takes us through examples dealing with all five physical senses. These are sight, sound, smell, taste and touch. It concludes with a sixth sense, which for the purposes of this book, I call intuition. Some may call it discernment, conscience, gut, knowing,

RED FLAG!

perception or feeling. It is a sense that you cannot put your finger on but it is just as real as any other.

RED FLAG!

Subsection A: Sight
Scenario #1

Client: "I'm considering leaving a church that I really love..."

Counselor: "Help me understand that. What would make you leave a church you really love?"

Client: "Rodney is this super friendly guy there but he creeps me out. Every time I see him I just get nervous. I want to run and cry at the same time?"

Counselor: "Is he bothering you? Is there security at the church?"

Client: "Well it's not like that. He's not really bothering me but it's just something about him that makes me uneasy."

Counselor: "Describe him to me."

Client: "Well, he looks just like my ex-boyfriend..."

Counselor: "Was your ex-boyfriend scary?"

Client: "Yes. One night after we broke up, he broke into my house and started punching me. I woke up in excruciating pain and the first thing I could clearly see was his face. He told me that if he couldn't have me then no one could."

Counselor: "Do you think Rodney is the same type of person your ex-boyfriend is?"

Client: "I don't think so. It's just that he could be his twin! My nightmares startup again after each time I see him at church."

Counselor: "Ok. Well, before you leave a church you love, let's see if we can work through this."

What is the trigger? The sight of this guy brings up painful memories. Because the guy at church looks like the abusive ex-boyfriend, she is triggered every week. His appearance makes her feel like her life may be in danger. Even though the guy at church is probably harmless, she does not feel that way when she's around him.

How do you possibly work through it? The trauma of the abuse is still present. The need for safety and security are of utmost importance. She may want to let the guy at church know how he affects her and why. Often, admitting the symptoms makes sense of them so that you can begin to heal from them. Then she must decide if she needs to distance herself from him while she works on her issues or whether she can utilize him in her process. A person who has attempted to take your life is not likely someone you will ever confront unless it's in a courtroom. However, you can use a stand in.

Another method of helping you resolve an issue like this is to write a letter to your abuser. This is not something you would likely ever mail. It's just a tool for you to use so that you can speak to him in whatever tone and whatever words you need to use to get rid of those feelings without the threat of retaliation. You could also simulate a scenario of you talking to him by using a counselor or a friend in his place. Find a way to confront him without putting yourself in harm's way. Then move forward without looking back. Do not do this work without a support system.

RED FLAG!

Scenario #2

Client: "I went to see a movie this weekend and had a meltdown."

Counselor: "What movie did you see?"

Client: "It was the *Black Panther*. But, it wasn't so much the movie as it was what happened in the theatre."

Counselor: "What happened?"

Client: "One side of the theatre was all white folks and on the other side was the blacks. It felt like I was a girl again. I got confused and didn't know whether I was gon' be allowed to sit down or not."

Counselor: "What did you do?"

Client: "My husband just took me by the hand and led me to our seats."

Counselor: "Were you able to enjoy the movie?"

Client: "After a little while I calmed down and I was able to pay attention."

What is the trigger? Seeing a segregated movie theatre was a trigger for this older woman. She grew up in an era where whites and blacks were legally separated and she was not allowed to go in some areas due to her skin color. This scenario was not set up by the theatre. As people came in they likely separated themselves for some reason. It may have been a matter or comfort or just coincidence. Whatever the case, this scene caused a regression in the woman. She literally became confused and did not remember that she could actually sit anywhere she wanted. She was transported in her mind back to a time where she couldn't.

How do you possibly work through it? One idea may be to return to the movies on a different day and see the same movie again. It is not likely that she will find the same scenario. She must remind herself that she has gone to plenty of movies before where this has never happened or even crossed her mind. She must remind herself that she is not back in those days. This is not that. However, because of the racial tensions going on our society today it may be difficult for some to differentiate. Talk this out with someone. You must try not to begin generalizing so that this becomes only an isolated incident in your mind. You want to stop this from spreading to the point where you are afraid to go back to the theatre or anywhere else. But, do realize that this concern may stick with you for a while. This incident was

RED FLAG!

traumatizing because of your mind and body's reaction to it. Do not pretend it didn't happen, but push yourself to remember all the other times you went to the same theatre without so much as a second thought.

RED FLAG!

Scenario #3

Client: "I've been having nightmares."

Counselor: "Do you remember the dreams once you wake up?"

Client: "Yes. It's like I'm reliving my dad beating up my mom all over again."

Counselor: "When did the nightmares start?"

Client: "A couple of weeks ago."

Counselor: "Did anything happen a couple of weeks ago out of the ordinary?"

Client: "The only thing I can think of is that I went to this party and saw this guy hit his girlfriend. Yeah…after that is when I started having the nightmares!"

What is the trigger? The sight of seeing someone being hit at a party triggered memories of his mom being hit when he was a kid. Something he thought he had gotten over suddenly began recurring in his dreams.

How do you possibly work through it? He must be honest with himself about whether or not he has truly processed and resolved his issues with what he saw growing up. If he hasn't, there is some work he needs to do. He may decide to offer his mother a safe place to get away to if she is still alive. If she has passed away, he may be able to put his mind at peace knowing that she is no longer in danger. There may be some feelings of shame and guilt that he is carrying because of being unable to help her when he was a child. He must work through understanding that it was not his fault and there was nothing he could have done. If his father is still alive he may decide to confront him. If he has passed away, he may just have to take comfort in knowing that he will not be able to hurt his mother nor anyone else anymore. He must then settle it within himself that he will not allow the issues of his father to continue to carry over into his own life. He may also decide whether or not he feels like there is something he can do for other women going forward. He has to consider that if he sees another man beating another woman, if there is something that he would do differently.

RED FLAG!

Subsection B: Sound
Scenario #1

Client: "I can't take it anymore! I'm scared all the time for no reason!"

Counselor: "What's going on? What are you scared of?"

Client: "The other day I heard a car backfire and I completely froze in front of all my friends!"

Counselor: "Ok. That sounds like your freeze mechanism engaged. It's a protective measure. When most people are scared or threatened they either fight, flight or freeze."

Client: "It didn't faze my friends at all. They just turned to look at the car. Why was I scared?"

Counselor: "I'm not sure. What did the backfire sound like to you and how close was it?"

Client: "The car was sitting in front of the next house and it sounded like a gunshot."

Counselor: "Weren't you standing fairly close to your mother when she was shot and killed?"

Client: "Yes, but that was over 20 years ago. I was

just a kid."

Counselor: "I understand that. But, what was your response when it happened?"

Client: "I was so scared that I didn't want to move. I didn't know what to do. I was frozen."

What is the trigger? The sound of the car backfiring was similar enough to the sound of a gunshot that it triggered the same response he had as a kid. His friends did not respond in the same way because they did not have the same experience. A trigger does not have to be an exact replica of the trauma. It only has to be close enough.

How do you possibly work through it? At this point, he must ask himself if he has dealt with his mother's death and the trauma surrounding it. If he hasn't then now is the time. He must dig deep and get honest. Get the help you need so that this issue does not continue to hinder you. You have to understand that it does not make you crazy because this is a trigger for you. However, it does make you different. You cannot stay away from all noises and sounds because that is impossible. The truth is, you may have this experience many more times. If at all possible, prepare yourself for places that you will go where there is a possibility of loud

RED FLAG!

noises. If you can wear earplugs to lessen the impact you may choose to do that. Let at least one person you are with know what you are dealing with. There is no need to be embarrassed. Everyone has their own issues to deal with. Learning relaxation techniques would also be helpful.

RED FLAG!

Scenario #2

Client: "I know something's wrong with me but I don't know what it is."

Counselor: "What makes you say that?"

Client: "Well...I was at work the other day and all of a sudden I went into a fit."

Counselor: "What do you mean by 'a fit'? Describe to me what happened."

Client: "I started getting nervous and agitated so I got up to go to the bathroom. Once I felt a little better I came back to my desk. But, about five minutes later I went and knocked her clock off her desk!"

Counselor: "Was the clock the problem or did she do or say something to make you angry?"

Client: "It was the clock. That damn ticking noise was about to drive me insane!"

Counselor: "Is that clock always on her desk or was it new?"

Client: "It was new. I can't stand clocks that tick! I only use digital clocks."

Counselor: "What bothers you about ticking clocks?"

Client: "I don't know…I just don't like the sound."

Counselor: "When was the last time you remember being near a ticking clock?"

Client: "At my grandma's house…in my uncle's bedroom…years ago."

Counselor: "What happened in your uncle's bedroom that made you hate that sound?"

Client: "He raped me to the tick of the clock like it was music or something…"

What is the trigger? The ticking sound of the clock took her back to being raped. She has avoided that sound for years so that she would not have to be reminded of a horrible time in her life. She did not connect the sound to the rape at first. She only knew that she didn't like it. Hearing it made her angry enough to act out of character in front of her co-workers.

How do you possibly work through it? Do not ignore past issues. If she has dealt with the rape at all, there may be parts of it that are still unresolved. It does not matter how long ago the trauma took place, a trigger brings it back to the present. She now realizes and remembers why she does not like the sound of a ticking clock. She must remind herself that no one is trying to hurt her and that she is safe. It is possible that other things that make similar sounds may trigger a reaction as well. Now that she is aware she can better prepare herself. She can now ask her co-worker to put her clock in a different location where she is unable to hear it. She can inform the people who are closest to her that she does not like anything that makes that type of sound. These modifications will not need to be in place forever. Just until she works through the trauma.

RED FLAG!

Scenario #3

Client: "I have to move out of my apartment immediately!"

Counselor: "What's happening with your apartment?"

Client: "My neighbors are just too loud. I'm on edge all the time."

Counselor: "What is it that puts you on edge? Are you bothered by any loud noise?"

Client: "No...not any loud noise. Just arguing. I can't stand it."

Counselor: "Have you gone to management or asked them to keep it down?"

Client: "No! If I complain they might hurt me."

Counselor: "What makes you think they would hurt you? Are they violent?"

Client: "Not yet..."

Counselor: "Is it possible that they don't realize how loud they are."

Client: "Maybe...but I still don't want to complain?"

Counselor: "Management could maintain your anonymity and just talk to them. It might calm things down."

Client: "That never happened in my house."

Counselor: "What happened in your house?"

Client: "Once an argument started between my parents it came to blows! A few times the police came and that always made my dad more angry. He always assumed I called them and then he would come after me! That's why I would never complain on my neighbors. It might get worse if I say anything."

What is the trigger? The sound of people raising their voices triggers him to go back to his childhood home where he witnessed domestic violence. If anyone tried to intervene, he was blamed and punished. Now he's in a situation where he is intimidated in his own apartment and feels the need to move out because he does not know how to handle it. Raised voices in his household ultimately lead to physical violence so he now assumes that this is simply what happens in every case.

RED FLAG!

How do you possibly work through it? He must conquer his fear of raised voices as well as his fear of taking action. He was taught to fear this type of situation because of the consequence he received when his father assumed he called for help. If he is unable to become more assertive he will likely run away for the rest of his life. He must identify what feels safe to him. Realizing that he is no longer a child under his father's roof is key. Understanding that he has options and choices that he can make is necessary. He must understand how his mind is generalizing what happened in his family to every similar situation. Even though he has never heard the neighbors become physically violent, he assumes they will eventually because that's what happened between his parents. Not everyone operates in the manner that his mother and father did. Learning conflict resolution would be a good idea for him. Not that he would step in and diffuse the arguments between his neighbors, but so that he can build confidence in himself. He needs to know that he can handle a situation without running and without being intimidated.

RED FLAG!

Subsection C: Smell
Scenario #1

Client: "I freaked out in the mall over the weekend and I have no idea what happened!"

Counselor: "Let's backtrack. Take me through your day up to that moment, starting with how you felt when you woke up."

Client: "It was really just a normal day. At least I didn't notice anything unusual. I got up, ate breakfast and got dressed. Then, I went to pick up my friend and went to the mall."

Counselor: "Do you remember what you were doing or where you were in the mall when the incident happened?"

Client: "We were in the men's section in the department store. I was standing there waiting for her to buy something for her husband. The last thing I remember was this guy walking by and right after that I started hyperventilating. I thought I was about to do die!"

Counselor: "Do you remember anything about the man? What he looked like, what he was wearing, his cologne?"

Client: "Oh my gosh! His cologne! He was wearing Eternity! I hate the smell of it!"

Counselor: "Why do you hate the smell of Eternity?"

Client: "He was wearing it..."

Counselor: "Who is he?"

Client: "My cousin. He raped me when I was 17. He always wore Eternity."

What is the trigger? The smell of a specific cologne is the trigger in this scenario. This client was raped by her cousin who always wore Eternity cologne. Since the rape, any time she smells this cologne she is triggered and is taken back to that place of fear and pain.

How do you possibly work through it? Ensuring that she has healed from being raped is the first step. If she "freaked out" in the mall over the scent of the cologne, there may be some lingering issues that she may have thought were already resolved. You may use a method of desensitization to change your perception of the scent. For instance, you could have a male that you know and trust well to intentionally wear the cologne when he's around you. This would be something

RED FLAG!

you would plan. It would not be something he would spring on you and just pop up wearing it. Do this in a safe environment on each occasion. You may be able to become less sensitive to the smell because someone you trust wears it often. Then, you can begin to associate the smell with someone familiar and safe. However, do not try this technique without having a mental health professional involved. Therapy should accompany the healing process. There could be other triggers that present themselves.

RED FLAG!

Scenario #2

Client: "My husband said I needed to see someone…"

Counselor: "What would make him say that? What happened?"

Client: "I came home from work the other day and he was baking chicken and I went off!"

Counselor: "What did you do when you 'went off'?"

Client: "I called my mom on the phone immediately and I started screaming for my children."

Counselor: "What were you afraid of? Was everyone alright?"

Client: "Everyone was fine and I really don't know why that happened. I haven't done that before. I felt like I did when I was a kid."

Counselor: "How did you feel when you were a kid?"

Client: "I was scared all the time because my dad was crazy!"

Counselor: "What do you mean by crazy? What would he do?"

Client: "He used to beat the crap out of my mom and then he would cook for us. He would beat her so bad that she couldn't get out of bed. Then I guess he felt bad because us kids wouldn't have any dinner."

Counselor: "What did he usually make for you guys to eat?"

Client: "The only thing he knew how to make was baked chicken…"

What is the trigger? The smell of baked chicken sent her back to a horrifying experience in her past. Even more so, was the fact that her husband was baking it. Whenever her father would abuse her mother, he made baked chicken for the children to eat because her mother was unable to move. Walking in to the smell of chicken baking in her home took her back. She feared for her mother and her children in that moment. It was just like she feared for her mother and her siblings when she was a child. Although her husband had never hurt her, the fact that he was baking chicken sent her to a place she had not been with him before.

RED FLAG!

How do you possibly work through it? She must understand that although she has grown up and gotten away from her father, she may fear that her mother is still in danger. She needs to examine her current life and honestly ensure that she is not in an abusive relationship with her own husband. If she is safe, then she has to begin to process and resolve the issues of fear due to the trauma she experienced as a child. She must admit that those fears exist and she will have to share the reality of this with her family, at least with her husband. She cannot go through this in silence or secrecy. Her freedom will be in releasing herself from the torment. If her mother is not safe, she may work with her on a safety plan. But, her focus is not her mother. It's her own healing.

RED FLAG!

Scenario #3

Client: "I had to pump my own gas over the weekend and I haven't been able to drive since."

Counselor: "What bothers you about pumping your own gas?"

Client: "I don't like the smell. I was in a car accident and the car caught fire."

Counselor: "Did you drive here today?"

Client: "No. My husband drove me."

Counselor: "Did you realize you had been traumatized by the car accident?"

Client: "Yes but I didn't know it was this big of a deal. My husband always pumps the gas for me. It was just that he was out of town this weekend."

Counselor: "Did your husband always pump your gas or did he start after the accident?"

Client: "He did it most of the time before but not always. I only pumped it once after the accident. He was with me that day and he told me he would do it for me after that.

Counselor: "Do you remember anything that happened the day you tried to do it?"

Client: "He said I was just standing at the pump like I was in a daze. I don't remember that though."

Counselor: "With trauma, it's not unusual to forget or to block things out. Are you ready to look into this and start dealing with it?

Client: "I don't know. I mean…I didn't know it was there and I don't understand it."

Counselor: "It sounds like you haven't worked through the trauma the accident caused you. There are plenty of people who don't like the smell of gas. But, it doesn't shut down their lives if they smell it. It certainly doesn't keep them from driving."

What is the trigger? The smell of gas triggers the trauma of the car accident. She seems to not really remember the details of the accident or how it has affected her. She just remembered that she smelled gas and it caught fire. The gas station may not be the only place that she will ever smell gas. She could be at a bar-b-que and have an episode if they are cooking with a gas grill.

RED FLAG!

How do you possibly work through it? She may need to pull her husband in on her treatment to help identify what happened the first time she tried to pump gas after the accident. There may also be other things that she does not remember that he can help with. She may need to process the accident itself. We do not typically see fires on a regular basis, but it is likely that seeing something on fire will have the same effect as the smell of gas. Her husband has attempted to protect her from her trauma up until this weekend when he was unavailable. There are portions of the treatment that she will need to do alone in order not to become dependent on her husband to cope for her. You will have to be ready for this because many times you will relive the incident in order to process it. This could cause additional trauma especially if there are details that you have forgotten. Do not do this without help.

RED FLAG!

Subsection D: Taste
Scenario #1

Client: "I can't eat cereal anymore and I can't be around other people eating it either."

Counselor: "What do you mean? What happens now if you eat cereal?"

Client: "It makes me really sad and I feel sick."

Counselor: "When did this start?

Client: "Well, I haven't had any in over a year. I just tried to eat it a couple times over this week."

Counselor: "Did anything significant happen around this time a year ago?

Client: "My dad died…"

Counselor: "What made you decide to try to eat cereal again after a year?"

Client: "I don't know. I just got a taste for it and decided to eat it."

Counselor: "Was that what you were doing when your dad died? Eating cereal?"

Client: "Actually…yes. That's exactly what I was doing when the hospital called to tell me he was gone."

What is the trigger? The trigger is the taste and possibly the act of eating the cereal. She began to associate eating cereal with the death of her father because that's what she was doing when she found out that he had died. She likely felt sick to her stomach and most certainly, overwhelmingly sad when she got that phone call. Eating cereal is still triggering her mind to go back to that moment on the phone when she got the disturbing call. There is nothing wrong with the cereal. However, a horrific thing happened while she was eating it so now those feelings are attached to it.

How do you possibly work through it? She must deal with the feelings of grief and sorrow that are still lingering after losing her father. It has only been a year since his death. There is no time limit on grief. She now needs a new association with cereal where there are no dark emotions attached. Have a cereal fight in the yard with the kids or grandkids. Make Christmas ornaments out of cereal. She should not shy away from the feelings she is still processing around the death of her father. However, preparation for a new way of doing things must also begin.

Scenario #2

Client: "I bit my tongue the other day and ever since I have been so calm. My anxiety has diminished."

Counselor: "Do you remember now why you were so anxious?"

Client: "No but I was scared of everything. Nobody could get near me or I was in a panic."

Counselor: "What was going on when you bit your tongue?"

Client: "Nothing really. I was chewing gum and just bit it."

Counselor: "Did it bleed?"

Client: "Yes it did. It was painful yet peaceful and I don't understand that."

Counselor: "Have you been cutting?"

Client: "No. I promised you I wouldn't and I haven't."

Counselor: "Was it the pain that gave you peace?"

Client: "It was the taste of blood. I felt like I didn't have to be scared anymore. At least for a little while."

Counselor: "What does the taste of blood remind you of?"

Client: "Getting beat up by my ex-boyfriend. He used to always ask me if I taste blood..."

Counselor: "Do you know why he would ask that?"

Client: "My punishment could only be over if I tasted blood. To him it meant that I would remember the beating. Once I tasted blood he would be satisfied and leave me alone."

What is the trigger? The taste of blood signified for her that her agony was over. Even if it was short-lived, she looked forward to it. She dealt with an intense, abusive relationship with her ex-boyfriend. She always knew that eventually she would have to take a beating for one reason or another. Much of her anxiety was caused by the anticipation of when the beating would come. After she had been beaten to the point of tasting blood, the anticipation was over. It was done and she could live freely for a while. She got used to the taste of blood signifying that her torment was

RED FLAG!

over.

How do you possibly work through it? This is not a way to live. This is likely one of the root causes of her self-harming behavior. Even after she got away from the ex-boyfriend, she began treating herself like he had. She must understand that no matter what, she does not deserve to be treated this way. No one should get away with harming her, not even her. She needs to find other ways to cope. Her self-esteem and self-worth have to be restored if it was ever there. If she never had love for herself then she will need to develop it. This takes spending time with herself. She has to learn to like herself so that she can understand how to love herself. Harm should not have to come so that she can find peace.

RED FLAG!

Scenario #3

Client: "I'm ready to start eating banana again."

Counselor: "What made you stop eating bananas?"

Client: "Well, not just bananas. I'm talking about anything with a banana flavor. It was my brother's favorite. After he died, every time I ate something that reminded me of him I just burst into tears."

Counselor: "What has made you ready now?"

Client: "I'm pregnant and it's like my baby is my brother reincarnated! The baby wants bananas and anything that tastes like it!"

Counselor: "Do you still cry when you eat it?"

Client: "Yes, but it makes my baby happy and it makes me feel close to my brother again. I want to do this now so that I'm not so emotional once the baby is born."

What is the trigger? The flavor of banana triggers sadness and memories of her deceased brother. Some triggers are obvious. We know exactly what it is, but it does not stop the emotional response. Pregnancy cravings do not care about your emotions. In this instance, her bringing a life into this world has warned her that she needs to take care of this trigger so that she can be as healthy as possible for her child.

How do you possibly work through it? When grieving, it's ok to be sad and no one can tell you how long your grieving process will be. Everyone is different. The taste of banana appears to be a fond memory she shared with her brother. The sadness comes from the fact that he is no longer physically available to share those times with. However, she now has a new life coming into the world that she may be able to have an even closer bond with. The baby in no way takes the place of her brother. Rather, it can be the bridge to helping her process through her pain. She must rid herself of any guilt she might feel for enjoying parts of her life without him. Reminding herself of the good times they had eating those things may be helpful. Knowing that since her brother loved it so much he would want her to go on continuing to enjoy it even without him. Making new memories with her baby while sharing the past memories of the brother she loved so much is bridging the loss. It's not a replacement. It is a way of keeping the essence of the person with you while letting go of the physical life that's now in the past.

RED FLAG!

Subsection E: Touch
Scenario #1

Client: "I need help communicating with people."

Counselor: "What do you think the problem is with your communication?"

Client: "When I'm face-to-face with people I am intimidated."

Counselor: "So, you are better at talking over the phone?"

Client: "Yes! When I communicate in writing or by phone I do just fine."

Counselor: "Describe for me what happens when you are talking with someone face-to-face."

Client: "I'm always watching their hands. I'm more focused on what they're doing than what they're saying."

Counselor: "Is it the movement of the other person that intimidates you?"

Client: "Um...well...I guess so."

Counselor: "Is it more of an attention thing? Are

you distracted by their movement or is it something else?"

Client: "I am distracted and the movement makes me nervous."

Counselor: "Is it more about the way they move or just the movement itself?"

Client: "I think it's just the movement itself."

Counselor: "Are you fearful they will hit you?"

Client: "Yes!"

Counselor: "Has anyone ever hit you while talking to you face-to-face?"

Client: "Of course! My dad used to hit me all the time. He did it to all of us. He used to say that we weren't worthy to stand toe-to-toe with him."

What is the trigger? The fear of being hit when standing "toe-to-toe" or face-to-face with someone is a trigger for this person. Why? Because it was done to her by her very own father. This behavior gave her a sense of feeling unworthy of talking to people in person, especially at close range. Anytime the person she was talking to would make a motion with their hands, it signaled a response to her that she needed to brace herself for impact or to get out of the way.

How do you possibly work through it? She must remind herself that she is no longer in front of her father. Self-esteem needs to be increased. She can practice face-to-face communicating with a counselor or friends and other family members where she feels safe to do so. She did not mention it but she likely has difficulty with eye contact as well. Understanding that you are just as worthy as anyone else to speak is important. Face-to-face communication techniques can be altered. Practice standing at an angle or beside the person you are speaking with instead of toe-to-toe. This posture can decrease tension and signal to both parties involved that this conversation is not meant to be confrontational. This way, if you're communicating with someone who is animated and talks with their hands, it doesn't feel like an attack.

RED FLAG!

Scenario #2

Client: "I need help with intimacy in my relationship."

Counselor: "What part of intimacy is a concern for you?"

Client: "I'm having a hard time being touched."

Counselor: "Are there any kind of touches that are ok?"

Client: "I like hugs and kisses but I don't like being squeezed."

Counselor: "You mean like a firm hug?"

Client: "No. I mean like squeezing my arm or leg or my hand. I hate holding hands!"

Counselor: "What does holding hands remind you of?"

Client: "My dad. He used to pretend that he was so in love with me or my mom and hold our hands in public."

Counselor: "What do you mean he would pretend to be in love with you?"

Client: "You know like a loving father might do. Hold his daughter's hand walking through the park or down the street. But, he was only doing it so he could squeeze it if I did something he didn't want me to do or said something he didn't want me to say."

Counselor: "So your boyfriend holding your hand feels like a punishment."

Client: "Yes!"

What is the trigger? The feel of a squeeze, especially on the hand is triggering past issues that are now intruding into her current relationships. The squeezing of her hand or another body part is signifying to her that someone is not being genuine as well as telling her that she should not be doing or saying something.

How do you possibly work through it? This is an issue that she most certainly needs to talk to her significant other about. Her father's affection was pretense and it angered her. She is now responding to others in the way she wishes she could have responded to her father. If she could have pulled her hand away from him she would have. Now, she can, however, it is causing a problem in her relationship. In this instance, she might ask the significant other to participate in at

RED FLAG!

least one counseling session with her. He needs to understand that when she rejects his advances that it's not really about him. She is reliving thoughts, feelings and emotions from the past and bringing them into the current. One thing that will be really important is to ensure that she is not dating someone who is just like her father. If she is, that's a problem in and of itself. She will not be able to heal from the pain of the past if she is repeating the cycle.

RED FLAG!

Scenario #3

Client: "My girlfriend just broke up with me a couple of weeks ago for no reason!"

Counselor: "She gave no indication that anything was wrong?"

Client: "Not at all! We were playing and she just jumped up and stormed out!"

Counselor: "What were you guys playing?"

Client: "I don't know...just playing... At the end I was tickling her."

Counselor: "She jumped up and ran out after you started tickling her?"

Client: "Yeah! She told me I was disgusting and that she hated me! Now she won't talk to me."

Counselor: "Did she say you touched her in a way that made her feel disgusting?"

Client: "No. I would never do that! Her uncle touched her when she was little. She told me about that so I would never do anything like that to her!"

Counselor: "I know you didn't intend to do anything that made her feel uncomfortable but it may have happened anyway. Did she ever tell you that her uncle tickled her?"

Client: "Aww man...yeah she did. That's exactly what she said he was doing right before he...I forgot all about that part."

What is the trigger? As harmless and as fun as tickling may be, it is a trigger for some. This client's girlfriend was molested by an uncle as a child and he apparently used tickling as a way to get her defenses down. It is likely that she had not thought about the molestation before they started playing the tickle game. She would not have necessarily thought to remind her boyfriend of such a thing either. She probably didn't even realize that it was a trigger for her.

How do you possibly work through it? In this case, the client would want to apologize in any way he can. He now has to realize that she did not break up with him because she didn't like him anymore. Even if he has to write her a letter or get a message to her through a mutual friend, he needs to let her know that he never meant to do anything to make her feel bad or uncomfortable. He might even let her know that he thinks he understands what happened and if she would like

RED FLAG!

to talk about it, he's available. Let her know that he is not angry with her and he still wants her in his life. After that, don't push. Hopefully, his girlfriend will accept his apology and realize that no matter where she is in her healing process, she may need a little more time and work. He may suggest they go to counseling together.

RED FLAG!

Subsection F: Intuition
Scenario #1

Client: "I need the right words to say to my sister. I just have no idea how to put it."

Counselor: "What happened? What is it that you need to tell her?"

Client: "She met a new friend and as soon as she walked in the room I knew I didn't like her."

Counselor: "How did you know that?"

Client: "My sister asked for her help with something and the friend answered. But, it was the way she answered."

Counselor: "Was it her tone of voice or body language?"

Client: "I'm not sure. I just knew that she was the kind of person that likes to take over. I can't stand that!"

Counselor: "Your sister didn't get the same kind of vibe from her?"

Client: "No. That's why I didn't say anything."

Counselor: "Do you feel like your sister needs to be warned?"

Client: "This girl wants something. I just don't know what it is."

What is triggering the insight? The vibe this particular person gave off struck the client in the wrong way. She has nothing to put her finger on. She just senses there is something to be concerned about with her sister's new friend. It could simply be a conflict in personality. If that's the case, this insight is only for the client. Her sister may not have the same conflict. However, what if there is something more?

How do you possibly handle a situation like this? This is difficult because there is nothing to pinpoint. It's a feeling the client has that her sister did not notice. Since nothing has really happened at this point, it may be that the client just watches the new friend. She could inform her sister that there is something about this new friend that she doesn't like. It does not mean her sister cannot or should not be friends with her, but it may allow the sister to be on alert. We will not always mesh well with everyone that our friends or family members mesh with. That's ok. If the client should see something concrete that she can bring to her sister's attention, she should do so. This gives the sister the option to make her own decision about whether or not she wants to continue the friendship.

RED FLAG!

Scenario #2

Client: "I'm really having a hard time at work and I feel like I might need to quit."

Counselor: "What's causing the difficulty? Is there not someone you can talk to in HR?"

Client: "No. That won't help. It's the atmosphere."

Counselor: "The atmosphere? Explain to me what happens when you walk into your office."

Client: "It feels dark and stuffy. Sometimes I just sit in the parking lot when I get to work."

Counselor: "What do you feel when you drive into the parking lot?"

Client: "I feel nervous and tired and I feel like crying."

Counselor: "Does this happen every day?"

Client: "Pretty much."

Counselor: "What do you think would make it better?"

Client: "I don't know. It feels like a dark cloud

comes to surround me as soon as I pull up. When I walk in it just smothers me."

What is triggering the insight? This could potentially be a toxic work environment for this client. In this case, it doesn't matter what anyone else is experiencing. If you are being consumed by darkness upon pulling up in your office parking lot, there is a problem for you.

How do you handle a situation like this? You must figure out whether or not it is the actual job causing the issue. Have you exhausted every avenue of trying to get any problems resolved that are going on in the workplace? Ask yourself if there is something going on in your personal life that is causing you to feel the way you are feeling or is it confined to the work environment? If your job is literally making you sick, eventually you will need to get out. Make an exit plan and follow it through. If it's being caused by another aspect in your life, you need a plan for how to deal with that as well. Do not try to ignore it. It will haunt you.

RED FLAG!

Scenario #3

Client: "There's this guy at church that I think is a child molester!"

Counselor: "What? What makes you think that about him?"

Client: "He has this look and walk about him. When he looks my way I just feel nasty…"

Counselor: "Have you ever seen him do anything inappropriate with a child?"

Client: "No. There's just something about him. He has some of the same characteristics as my uncle."

Counselor: "Is your uncle a child molester?"

Client: "Yup!"

Counselor: "What are the similarities you see between your uncle and the guy at church?"

Client: "There's just something about him that makes me feel like I need to take a shower after I've been anywhere near him. I feel like he just saw right past my clothes and pictured me naked. Just nasty!"

What is triggering the insight? Something about this guy reminds this client of her uncle who is a child molester. She could not seem to give great detail about the similarities except for the way he made her feel. But, for her that's enough.

How do you handle a situation like this? This is a delicate situation because you cannot just accuse someone from a feeling. You will need to keep your distance while watching at the same time. Do not harass him. He may be someone who is completely innocent but just reminds you of your uncle. However, if what you're feeling is correct, the children at the church are not safe. You may have to ask around. Does he work with the children or have access to them? Does the church run background checks on anyone working with children? They should. Do your due diligence inconspicuously and report anything concrete that you can bring to the church's attention. If you witness inappropriate behavior with a child, you can and should contact Child Protective Services yourself at 1-800-252-5400.

Message from the Author

I wrote this book because of the world we live in today. It seems that doing wrong has become the norm and doing what's right gets us outcasted. A world where talking about Jesus makes us "one of those". It is so easy to miss a sign of warning because someone trying to do you harm is expected. My counseling office is flooded with survivors of incest, rape and domestic violence. I am glad to see movement from victim to survivor, but now I want to see survivors move to an abundant life. A life where just existing is not enough and living is the only option. Let's learn how to better protect ourselves and others from being victimized. Let's stop being OK with or looking the other way when a loved one is being abused by their own hands or the hands of someone else. Know it when you see it and call it what it is...a RED FLAG!

About the Author

Soneakqua White, M.A., LPC has been in the mental health field for the past fourteen years. She received her Bachelor of Arts in Psychology from Baylor University in 1998. She completed a Master of Arts in Counseling from Amberton University in 2002. Her credential as a Licensed Professional Counselor (LPC) was granted by the Texas State Board of Examiners in January 2006. Soneakqua successfully transitioned into her practice, At the Table Counseling, in April 2011. She currently serves a large population of men and women who have suffered physical, verbal, mental/emotional, sexual and/or spiritual abuses in their youths. Her desire is to assist them by walking with them through their healing processes.

Other Books By Soneakqua J. White

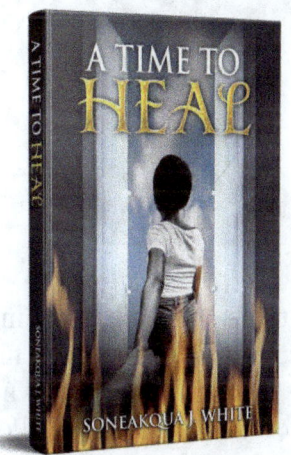

Get Connected

Facebook.com/AttheTableCounseling
Instagram.com/atthetablecounseling
Twitter.com/ATC_Counseling

Need More Help?

Author Soneakqua J. White has created an online course to assist you in your healing process. This course is designed to help you deal with a mother who makes it difficult for you to care *for* and/or care *about* her. If you have ever asked yourself "why does my mother treat me the way she does" this course is for you. If you have found yourself wanting to scream out "Help! My mom doesn't like me" this course is for you. If you spent the majority of your life trying to make your mother proud of you or just trying to survive being raised by her and you still have not succeeded…this course is for you. You will learn how to love yourself even though she didn't like you. You will learn to stop compromising your mental, physical, emotional and spiritual health to get someone to love you who does not acknowledge your effort. Take your power out of her hands and live! Copy the link below in your url to receive the coupon code for this course.

https://www.udemy.com/working-through-mommy-issues/?couponCode=DOTHEWORK

RED FLAG!

Resources

Rape, Abuse & Incest National Network (RAINN)
www.rainn.org
1-800-656-4673

National Domestic Violence Hotline
www.thehotline.org
1-800-799-7233

Legal Assistance
www.womenslaw.org
1-800-799-7233

National Suicide Prevention Lifeline
www.suicidepreventionlifeline.org
1-800-273-8255

Soneakqua J. White, M.A.,LPC-S
At the Table Counseling
www.atthetablecounseling.com

Substance Abuse and Mental Health Services Administration (SAMHSA)
www.samhsa.gov
800-662-4357

Get Briefed
Sexual Violence Support
www.letsgetbriefed.com
877-214-0988

www.ingramcontent.com/pod-product-compliance
Lightning Source LLC
Chambersburg PA
CBHW052021070526
44584CB00016B/1846